The Ultimate Guide to Homeschooling Boys

Michelle Caskey

IMP
Inquisitive
Minds Press

The Ultimate Guide to Homeschooling Boys

© 2015 Michelle L. Caskey. All rights reserved

Published by *Inquisitive Minds Press*®
Caledonia, MI 49316
www.InquisitiveMindsPress.com

Printed in the United States of America
ISBN-10:1515032795
ISBN-13:978-1515032793

All rights reserved. No part of this book may be reproduced, stored in a retrieval system, or transmitted in any form by any means – electronic, mechanical, photocopy, recording or otherwise – without prior permission of the publisher, except as provided by U.S. copyright law.

Cover by Michelle Caskey

Interior page layout by Michelle L. Caskey

This book is dedicated to my best friend and my biggest fan, Dennis Caskey. You believed in me when I didn't believe in myself. You encouraged me when I didn't think that writing a book was possible. You inspired me to make my dreams come true. I couldn't have done any of this without you, Sweetie. I love you!

Introduction.. 11

Understanding Our Boys
Surprise 15

Is Your Son's Brain Starving? 21

5 Reasons Why it's GOOD to Have a Strong Willed Son.... 27

Kids & Teens w/ Focusing, Attention, or Sensory Issues 35

Smart Kids Who Hate to Write.. 43

Yes, Your Child Will Learn to Read 51

How Much Media Should We Allow in our Homeschools?. 57

Important Training for Our Sons
13 Easy Ways to Fit Exercise into your Day 61

Turning our Boys into Men 65

4 Benefits from Allowing Your Child to Make Mistakes 67

5 Ways to Find Out What's in Your Son's Heart 73

Tangible Ways to Express Love to Your Son....................... 79

Do Your Words Inspire or Demoralize Your Children?....... 83

Conformed or Transformed? 89

5 Vital Things You Can Do to "Harden Off" Your Son....... 91

"I'm Never Going to Use This!".. 99

Increase their Attention Span... 105

Nurturing Competent Communicators................................. 111

Yes, Homeschoolers DO Experience Peer Pressure!.......... 115

The 5 Most Important Things to Teach Your Child 121

Getting Your Teenager to Wake Up in the Morning 125

Our Grand Experiment... 131

"You Were Right, Mom!"... 137

6 Important Considerations for Raising Engaged Citizens. 143

Teaching Techniques - General
Better Late Than Early?... 147

Four Questions to Avoid a One Size Fits All Education 151

Give Yourself a Break! 157

Develop a Motivation to Learn in Your Sons!..................... 161

Fun Elementary Lessons 167

How to Teach Your Son When He Won't Sit Still.............. 171

Ignite their Enthusiasm for Learning 177

Incorporate Games into their Lessons................................. 183

Teaching Boys 187

The Best Way to Learn 191

What To Do When Your Child Hits a Wall........................ 193

Evaluate Student Learning 197

Giving Your Children an Exemplary Education.................. 201

Teaching Techniques - Specific Subjects
Choosing Good Books 205

Reading Living Books vs Textbooks.................................. 209

Make Your Own Homeschool Preschool Curriculum 213

Making Math Marvelous.. 221

6 Ways to Get Boys to Consume the Classics 227

Homeschool Record Keeping 233

Homeschool High School Record Keeping 237

Homeschool Reading Program 241

13 Benefits of Unit Studies 247

Teach Your Boys How to Enjoy Studying History 253

Should We Stop Teaching Higher Level Math? 259

Bachelor's Degree by Age 18 265

Character Education Through Volunteering 273

The Benefits of Being a Student Entrepreneur 277

Outdoor Learning Activities 283

For Moms with Sons - Homeschooling Focus

How to Start Homeschooling 297

Are you Letting God Write Your Homeschool Story? 301

Are We Focused on the Right Things? 305

8 Tips for a Tired Homeschool Mom 309

Are We Frustrating Our Children? 313

Are You Discouraged? 319

Attention Perfect Homeschooling Moms 327

De-stressing 101 for Homeschool Moms 331

Homeschool: Am I Doing Enough? 335

Is Homeschooling Strengthening Your Marriage ? 341

Keeping Your Sanity in a Busy Homeschool World 347

Remembering What's Important 353

You Can't Have It All 357

7 MUST DO Homeschool End of Year Tasks 361

Attend a Homeschool Convention 365

The 5 Dangers of Attending Homeschool Conventions 369

What About Socialization? 373

What If the Kids Want to Go Back to School? 377

No Money for Vacation? 383

Rewards for Kids 387

Getting Dads More Involved with Homeschooling 393

Just Say No! 401

Stick With It 405

An Encouraging Word 411

Introduction

During the process of writing this book, I felt myself becoming convicted. When my boys were younger, I made it a point to provide hands-on lessons. I worked hard to be sure they were enjoying their schoolwork. When we first started homeschooling, my boys thought learning was fun.

Somehow, in the last several years, both of my boys have turned into young men. As I write this book, my oldest son is entering 10th grade in the fall and my youngest son is entering 8th grade. As their minds and bodies have been changing, my lessons for them have been changing as well.

As my boys left the fun, elementary school years I felt more and more pressure to conform their lessons to the type they would have had if they were in school.

I've been fearful that they might not be receiving as rigorous of an education as they would be if they were in school – and that has caused me to make their schoolwork harder and harder.

Somewhere in that process, both of my boys decided that they didn't like school anymore. They would rather do just about anything than their schoolwork. I'd just about resigned myself to the fact that most boys don't like school – so if my boys didn't like their lessons I shouldn't take it personally.

Then I read through some of the older articles on my blog. I heard myself say again and again that our children's minds are fires to be ignited and not vessels to be filled. I heard myself repeat how important it is for our kids to love the learning process. I heard myself emphasize how we need to take the time to do the hands-on projects, to try to reach our sons where they're at, and to do whatever it takes to make learning fun.

How did I lose the desire to do that for my boys? When did I start taking the easy way out? Why did I start introducing more textbooks into our homeschool?

I came to the realization that I have been institutionalized. As much as I've tried to fight it, I was a publicly schooled kid from K-12. Actually, I attended from K-16 because I have four years of public college under my belt as well.

As my boys got older, I started to think more about being sure they are prepared to go to college and get a job. I allowed my fears and uncertainties to taint my boys' homeschool experience. My boys stopped enjoying school. How heartbreaking!

As you read this book, know that I will also be planning our next school year with fresh eyes and a new determination.

Here are my new resolutions:
1. To be sure that God remains the center of our studies
2. To study each of my boys to learn what excites them at this age
3. To make next year's studies more enjoyable for my sons
4. To focus more on my sons' strengths and less on their weaknesses
5. To help each boy become the young man who God wants him to be

When it comes to learning, most boys don't want us to throw a workbook at them and walk away. Our boys require different teaching methods which may stretch us homeschool moms. However, once we've learned how to best reach our sons, homeschooling our boys can become an exciting adventure!

I'm eager to take these steps back to what I know is important:
- I will return to relying on God to ensure their future success rather than my boys' education.
- I will stop trying to rush my boys through my checklists each day.
- I will remember that character is more important than academics.
- I look forward to doing the messy, hard projects that my boys have always loved.
- I will do everything in my power to put the love back into learning!

I look forward to having you join me on this journey.

Michelle Caskey
www.homeschool-your-boys.com

Surprise

Your Son is Not a Girl!

We all know that boys and girls are different from each other. You may be surprised, however, to learn just how different they actually are.

Dr. Leonard Sax has written some eye-opening books on this topic called **Why Gender Matters**[1] and **Boys Adrift**[2]. I was amazed to learn that boys have a lot more physical and mental differences from girls than what we are normally taught. Dr. Sax includes scientific evidence in his books to show that boys not only behave differently than girls, they also hear differently, see differently, respond to stress differently, and think differently.

The things boys can learn are similar to what girls can learn; but, the way they go about learning is very different. Boys require a different educational environment and teaching approach if we are going to help them reach their full potential.

---

[1] Why Gender Matters by Dr. Leonard Sax
[2] Boys Adrift by Dr. Leonard Sax

Boys SEE Differently

Males have more rods in their eyes versus cones. Rods help us to see distance and speed. Females have more cones than rods. Cones help us to see color and shape. Because of this difference, boys tend to draw verbs with little color variation in their pictures while girls tend to draw nouns with lots of different colors.

> *Boys require a very different educational environment and teaching approach if we are going to help them reach their full potential.*

When asked to draw a picture, Sally will draw a house with people and flowers and lots of pretty colors. Steve will draw a tornado which is knocking down a house – and his picture will look like a large black swirl.

Implications for teaching boys

- Do not expect young boys to draw something recognizable or pictures with lots of colors. Be sure not to discourage boys by assuming they aren't putting forth as much effort as are girls just because they draw differently. When we find fault with them in this way, boys begin to think that art is for girls and not for boys.
- Allow them to draw verbs and to do it in a way that is fast and furious.
- Don't hold eye contact with a boy unless you're disciplining him.

Boys HEAR Differently

Baby girls can hear ten times better than boys, and this difference gets even more pronounced as they get older. Boys can only hear every 3rd word or so of soft-spoken teachers. When boys can't hear what their teacher is saying, they tend to drift off – which earns some boys the incorrect diagnosis of ADHD.

Boys also tend to make little noises wiggling and tapping pencils which are irritating to girls – but they don't even realize they are making them.

Implications for teaching boys

- Speak more loudly than you normally would and be very expressive.
- Use lots of voice fluctuation and hand motions to engage boys.
- While working with your son, sit down next to him, spread the materials out and look at them shoulder to shoulder.

Boys THINK Differently

We don't yet know all of the differences in how boys and girls think; but, we now know that their brains are arranged differently. We've all heard that we use the left side of our brain for verbal activities and the right side for art. Actually, we're starting to discover that this is only true in males.

Males who have had a stroke on the left side of their brain lose 80% of their verbal ability. The verbal ability in females who have a stroke on the left side of their brain is much less impacted, proving that their verbal ability is spread across both sides of their brain.

There are many other differences in how male and female brains are arranged. For more details, check out Dr. Sax's books.

Implications for teaching boys

- Book learning is essential; but, without practical, hands-on experience, boys will have a hard time grasping concepts that seem simple to us. They will disengage from their lessons.
- Boys need real world experiences in their education which engage all of their senses.
- Boys also need plenty of time outdoors.
- Boys have a hard time processing their emotions. Don't ask boys, "How would you FEEL if..." questions. Ask them, "What would you DO if..." questions.
- Boys like to have at least some control over their environments. Put each day's schoolwork into a folder and let them decide the order in which they will complete it.

When studying literature, try these tips:

- Have boys draw maps based on clues in the book.
- Assign articles from the daily newspaper.
- Have them read books with strong male characters doing unpredictable things (i.e., C.S. Lewis, Hemingway, Dostoevsky, Twain, etc.)

Boys SEE THEMSELVES differently

Girls tend to underestimate their own abilities. Boys tend to overestimate their own abilities. Boys also enjoy taking risks much more than do girls. The more a boy takes risks the more favorably he tends to be seen by his peers.

Danger itself gives boys a pleasant feeling of exhilaration as opposed to the fearful feelings it causes in girls. Moderate stress also helps boys to perform better as adrenaline causes more blood to flow to their brains. Stress has the opposite effect on girls.

Implications for teaching boys

- Boys respond well to a challenge if there are winners and losers.
- A competitive team format works better than individual competitions for boys because they don't want to let their teammates down.
- Participating in single-sex activities such as boy scouts or team sports are beneficial for your sons.

If your son seems to crave danger, take these necessary steps:

- Give him lessons with a professional (i.e., skiing instructor) to help him to more accurately evaluate his own abilities.
- Supervise your child. His risk is lower if he isn't allowed to be alone with groups of peers because he will be less likely to try to "show off" for his friends if an adult is present.
- Assert your authority – don't argue with your son. Don't negotiate. Just do what you have to do (i.e., lock up his bike.)

By the way, the optimum temperature for learning for boys is 69 degrees, while it is 74 degrees for girls. If you set the temperature so that it is comfortable for you, you may find your sons fall asleep or their minds wandering instead of focusing on their lessons.

It works well if you have the opportunity to set up a single-sex learning environment for your children. Try using different methods to teach your sons as opposed to the ones you use to teach your girls and you will be amazed at how your sons respond to your efforts!

Armed with this knowledge, we can set up more ideal learning environments where we can engage our sons and help them to reach their full potential.

Is Your Son's Brain Starving?

Most of us are aware that boys and girls are different. They see things differently, they play differently and they think differently. I was surprised to find out recently that boys also have different nutritional needs than do girls. Is your son's brain starving?

I recently had the privilege of attending several seminars by Dianne Craft , who is a special education teacher and a nutritionist. Dianne shared some information with us that I had never heard before. She told us that sixty percent of our brains are made of fat. Thirty percent of that fat is in the forebrain, which is made of DHA, an essential fatty acid. The only sources of DHA are fish oil and mother's milk.

Diane told us that we all need healthy fats in our diets to make our brains function properly. The corpus collosum, which is the bundle of nerves that connects the right and left hemispheres, is made of fat. The myelin sheath which coats the nervous system is also made of fat.

Boys have a 3 times higher need for essential fatty acids than do girls. Dianne believes this is because estrogen is a fatty carrier where testosterone is not. This also explains why it's so much easier for men to lose weight than women. What is an asset for weight loss, however, is not an asset for their brains. Some of our sons are suffering from brain starvation.

Our modern diets are deficient in good fats. We are told to eat margarine instead of butter, egg beaters instead of eggs, skim milk instead of whole milk, and to stay away from nuts because they are high in fat. A lack of essential fatty acids causes our bodies to become deficient in serotonin.

Serotonin has the following beneficial mental effects:
- Creates a natural, antidepressant release in the body
- Relaxes the mind
- Instills a sense of well-being
- Helps us handle stress
- Keeps our mind focused
- Promotes good sleep patterns
- Helps us to have a positive outlook on life
- Helps us control our impulses

Our society is becoming more and more deficient in serotonin. There are more people on anti-depressants than ever before. Children are being put on Ritalin and other psychotropic drugs at an alarming rate. Dianne informed us that Ritalin works by releasing serotonin in the body. If parents knew that they could help to positively affect their child's body chemistry in a more natural way, do you think they would elect to put their child on drugs which may have harmful side effects? I think not.

How do you know if your child is deficient in DHA?

Mental symptoms of DHA Deficiency include the following:
- Hyperactivity
- ADD
- Impulsivity
- Anxiety

- Anger
- Sleep problems

Physical symptoms of DHA Deficiency include the following:
- Dry hair
- Dry skin
- Cracks in ends of fingers
- Chapped lips
- Excessive thirst
- Warts
- Glare sensitivity
- Poor vision

If your child exhibits any of these mental and/or physical symptoms, he would be a great candidate for trying to increase his intake of essential fatty acids.

The left hemisphere of our brain is where our judgment resides. It is the logical part of the brain. Our right hemisphere is where our emotion resides. When boys aren't using good judgment, they are having a difficult time accessing their left hemisphere.

Sometimes, this is due to a lack of essential fatty acids. Information can't travel across the corpus collosum if it isn't nourished properly. The solution is for us to fatten up their brains!

So, how do we fatten up our boys' brains?

Dianne Craft recommends the following nutritional regimen:

1. Increase their intake in EFA – EFA stands for essential fatty acids, which are also known as polyunsaturates or "good fats." There are two types:
- **Omega-6**, which is found in raw nuts, seeds, legumes and unsaturated vegetable oils such as sesame.

- **Omega-3**, which is found in flaxseed oil, walnut oil, and deep-water fish.

If your children don't eat any of these foods, as mine don't, you will want to get these nutrients from supplements. Exact supplements and dosages are detailed in Dianne's ***Biology of Behavior***[3] CD set.

2. Try to increase protein – Be sure your children eat protein throughout the day to help stabilize their mood. Try to make breakfast high in protein.

These are good, higher protein food choices:
- Nuts and seeds
- Eggs and sausage
- Real butter
- Real mayonnaise
- Whole milk
- Tuna and mayonnaise
- Protein shakes
- Smoothies with protein powder in them
- Real peanut butter (natural so it isn't loaded with sugar)
- Cheese and crackers
- Have dinner for breakfast

Boys usually love to have lots of butter and mayonnaise on their food because they're craving the fat. These condiments help to balance their body chemistry. Let them have it!

3. Try to limit sugar and sugary carbs – Sugar tears down the adrenal gland which drains our energy and causes us to go into fight or flight mode much too easily. You don't want to become the food police; however, try to do what you can to lessen the

---

[3] Biology of Behavior (CD) by Dianne Craft

amount of sugar your kids are eating. Fill them up on the protein rich, fatty foods instead and they won't have as much room for the sugar. By the way, carbs such as cereal, waffles, pancakes, etc. make us tired so it is best to eat them at night.

While some children do require medications in order to change their body chemistry, there are also children who do not. Try making one change per week to your son's diet and watch the results. Having the right essential fatty acids in your child's brain will literally change their body chemistry. You may be amazed at the positive changes that you observe in your son.

Our family has been following these and other tips from Dianne for several months and we've definitely noticed a difference in all of us. We are all calmer, we are sleeping better, and there seems to be a lot less anxiety around our house.
Dianne has many other excellent suggestions as well! For more information, check out Dianne Craft's website[4]. I would also highly recommend purchasing her ***Biology of Behavior*** CD set.

---

[4] www.diannecraft.org

5 Reasons Why it's GOOD to Have a Strong Willed Son

By the time my oldest son turned 13-year-old, he had been arguing with us about everything for a couple of years. Even the most benign requests from us were usually met with questions about why he should comply. Dealing with his behavior became exhausting and frustrating! I started thinking that he'd better grow up to be a lawyer so that at some point he would get paid to argue… and he'd be arguing with someone else!

My husband and I have been dealing with our strong willed sons' behavior since they were little. In a study of 35,000 parents which was conducted by James Dobson, it was discovered that there are nearly three times as many strong willed kids as there are compliant kids. And there is a slight tendency for males to be strong willed over females. Also, if you have a strong willed son, there's a 92% chance that you knew about it before your child was 3 years old.

According to that study, if you have more than one child, you probably have at least one who is strong willed.

As I said before – we have two strong willed sons... but our older son is even stronger willed than his younger brother. One of the most vivid examples I can remember of dealing with their strong willed behavior was when my oldest son was about two years old. I had driven him to the mall to get his picture taken; however, once we got there, he refused to sit for the session. The photographer and I tried to bribe and cajole him as much as we could... but my son flat out refused to comply.

We finally gave up, and I walked back to the car with my now calm son. As we started to climb into the car, he decided he wanted to go back and have his picture taken after all. There had been a long line of people waiting behind us and I explained to him that our turn was over. We couldn't go back in now.

After hearing that, my son threw a huge temper tantrum. This wasn't a regular toddler tantrum. He was flailing at me, bucking like a bronco, and he refused to let me buckle him into his car seat. I remember having to spend 20 minutes trying to push him down into his car seat enough that I could get him strapped in.

I'm sure that everyone who walked by in the parking lot thought I was an abusive mom. There was nothing I could do to get him to stop screaming. It was an extremely humiliating moment. I felt powerless!

Fortunately, my boys don't throw temper tantrums quite like this now that they're older... However, once they get an idea into their heads, they're like Dobermans who have their teeth sunk deep into a meaty bone – and they won't let go for anything!

I recently heard a podcast by Hal and Melanie Young, authors of Raising Real Men called *Transitioning to Adulthood*[5].

In this podcast, Hal and Melanie Young interviewed Israel Wayne, homeschool graduate and father of seven. He is also the author of ***Homeschooling from a Biblical Worldview***[6] and ***Full-Time Parenting: A Guide to Family-Based Discipleship***[7]. In this podcast, they discussed why it's good that our teenage sons question our authority. Yes, you read that correctly.

Being strong willed can be a positive trait. That fact, however, doesn't mean that it's easy for us parents to deal with!

Here are 5 reasons why questioning our authority can be good:

1. Strong willed sons are more likely to reach their full potential – Compliant kids have a hard time standing up for themselves and voicing their opinions. This makes them vulnerable to the whims of their peers and to others who may not have their best interests at heart.

2. Questioning helps kids to internalize values – Your strong willed son wants to learn things for himself rather than just accept what others say as truth.

This is obviously an excellent trait. He won't be swayed back and forth by whatever opinions are floating around him.

---

[5] Transitioning to Adulthood (podcast) by Hal and Melanie Young
[6] Homeschooling from a Biblical Worldview by Israel Wayne
[7] Full-Time Parenting: A Guide to Family-Based Discipleship by Israel Wayne

3. It's a natural part of transitioning to adulthood – Most boys are going to question our authority at some point. It's better for this to happen when they are 13-15 rather than waiting until they're older. They may pitch a fit; but, there aren't many other options open to them at the younger age. If they don't rebel until they're older, and have access to a car or are away at college, their rebellion can destroy their life and/or the lives of others.

4. They're coming to you to sort through information – It's much better for your son to come to you with his concerns than to be outwardly compliant but is secretly rebelling when he isn't in your presence. Be glad that he made the effort to let you know what's going on in his mind.

5. If handled correctly, it will strengthen your relationship – While our kids are transitioning from childhood to adulthood our role as their parent also needs to be adjusted. We need to slowly shift our role from benevolent dictator to trusted adviser. This will help to ensure that our sons will continue to feel comfortable talking with us throughout their adult years.

Hal and Melanie remind us that there is a difference between our sons questioning us and full blown rebellion. As long as their tone is respectful, we need to encourage our sons' questions.

> *We need to slowly shift our role from benevolent dictator to trusted adviser.*

Questions are normal and healthy. We shouldn't view them as a challenge to our authority. We want our kids to know that they

can always come to us with disagreements and that we'll be alright with it. Kids need a safe place to talk through various issues. If we aren't that safe place then they will find someone else to talk with instead.

Even though it's good to have a strong willed son, it isn't easy.

Here are 8 tips which should help when parenting a strong willed son:

1. Give him choices – Instead of always telling your son what to do, give him several options you're okay with and let him choose. The more he feels like he has some control over his decisions, the less likely he will feel like he needs to try to wrestle control away from you in areas where you want his compliance.

2. Let him learn – Strong willed kids learn through experience. These are the boys who need to touch the hot stove to believe that it will burn them. Be prepared that these kids will test your limits. Sometimes, just knowing why they are acting a certain way will take some of the sting out of their behavior. Don't take it personally. Try to be understanding.

3. Don't create power struggles – There are definitely areas where our kids need to listen and obey. There are other areas where it really doesn't matter which choice our child makes. If you draw hard lines in every area of life, these kids will often defy you just to prove a point. If it isn't a sin issue, consider whether you might want to bend in the area of contention.

4. Let him have opinions – Your son DOES need to obey but he doesn't have to like it. If your son is acting respectfully but is just not overjoyed about what he has to do, don't pick at him about it. Allow him to have his own feelings. Sometimes a cooling off period is necessary before attitudes will be good again.

5. Ask him questions – When your son has an issue with something you've asked him to do, ask him why? Try to understand his point of view. When we listen to our sons, we will often find that they have some good points!

6. Be willing to apologize – Sometimes our kids are mad because they've asked us to do something and we've forgotten about it. Or we don't handle a situation very well. Once your child expresses their frustration, be willing to listen to what he's saying. If you are at fault, be quick to admit it. Being humble in this way does more to repair a relationship than just about anything else.

> *If it isn't a sin issue, consider whether you might want to bend in the area of contention.*

7. Respect your son – Strong willed kids often fight us because they feel disrespected. If your child wants to do something you don't want him to do, try to understand where he's coming from.

If he feels understood he will be less likely to have a desire to fight you over every little issue.

8. Get dad involved – Once your son is around age 12, he will have a hard time "taking orders" from mom. During this time, it is much easier for a son to obey his father than it is for him to take direction from his mother. When you sense that friction arising, ask your husband to step in and deal with the situation.

Parenting a strong willed son is hard work!

Once you realize what's happening in your child's mind, however, hopefully that will go a long way toward making the journey a little bit less difficult.

Even though individual days and weeks can pass slowly for us parents, the years do fly by. If you make the effort to build a solid relationship with your strong willed son now, you will reap the benefits of seeing him grow into a successful man later.

Kids & Teen with Focusing, Attention, or Sensory Issues

A few years ago, I was blessed to be able to hear some amazing talks by someone named Dianne Craft. Dianne has a master's degree in special education, she's a certified nutritional health professional, and she was a homeschool mom. She has a heart for helping kids who are often labeled as having attention deficit issues.

How do you know if your child has focusing, attention, or sensory issues? Do you have a child with the following:

- He appears to have to work hard to stay focused on a task.
- He instantly stops working as soon as you leave the room.
- It takes him a long time to complete his work.
- He seems lazy and unmotivated.

If these statements describe your child there is hope. Your son may be suffering from a low level of serotonin.

Diane has some common sense advice which might be surprising to you. **Not all of these kids need to be medicated!**

It takes lots of energy to stay focused on something which isn't interesting to you. If your son's body isn't producing enough serotonin, his ability to focus will be greatly impaired. Serotonin is a neurotransmitter which is mostly manufactured in the gut or intestines.

Serotonin has the following beneficial effects:
- Relaxes the mind
- Instills a sense of well-being
- Helps us handle stress
- Keeps our mind focused
- Promotes falling asleep and staying asleep through the night
- Is an antidepressant
- Helps us control impulses
- Gives us a more positive outlook on life

You can see how a lack of serotonin would put a real burden on a child's system. Many of the kids who exhibit the above symptoms are put on Ritalin or some other psychotropic drug in order to help with these behaviors.

Ritalin works by helping our bodies to release serotonin. It also has 23 side effects, some of which are quite dangerous. As of 2010, according to the National Health Interview Survey, 8.4 percent, or 5.2 million children, between the ages of 3 and 17 had been given diagnoses of attention deficit hyperactivity disorder.

My boys have never struggled with their ability to focus. In fact, I almost missed going to this talk of Dianne's because I didn't think I needed to hear it. Little did I know that a lack of serotonin can also cause all sorts of sensory issues as well. Take a look at the various issues which can be caused by sensory processing problems:

Auditory Sensory Processing Symptoms:
- Sensitive to loud noises
- Dislikes being in a group
- Language was delayed

Taste Sensory Processing Symptoms:
- Food textures bother them
- Won't eat meat
- Chews on clothing
- Very selective eater (carbivore)
- Foods can't touch on plate

Touch Sensory Processing Symptoms:
- Clothing tags bother them
- Socks have to have soft seams
- Dislikes non-soft clothing such as jeans

Loud noises have always bothered both of my sons. They actually bother myself and my husband as well! My oldest son also had a tendency to chew on the neck of his shirt, he needed me to cut the tags off of all of his shirts, and he was a carbivore. Both of my sons had struggled with several of the other issues as well.

Once Dianne gave out these symptoms I was definitely listening. I thought these were character traits in my sons – I had no idea that they were symptoms for which we might be able to give them some relief.

Dianne said that she researched to find out what was going on in these kids that could cause them to have these symptoms. She came across a study done by different doctors, one of whom was Dr. Leo Galland, author of **Superimmunity for Kids**[8] and **Power Healing**[9]. He attributed these and other behaviors to something called "leaky gut." He said that when your gut doesn't contain the right amount of beneficial bacteria your body will not produce as much serotonin as it should. Also, the yeast in your system can grow out of control.

Having an upset gut ecology causes the following symptoms:

Behavioral Characteristics of Upset Gut Ecology:
- Mood Swings
- Spaciness
- Anger/irritability/aggression
- Inconsistent performance
- Inattention
- Sensory Processing Issues
- Depression
- Asperger's and Autistic-like behaviors
- Memory problems (math facts, spelling, etc.)
- Inappropriate behavior such as talking loudly, getting into other people's space, etc.

---

[8] Superimmunity for Kids by Dr. Leo Galland
[9] Power Healing by Dr. Leo Galland

Physical Characteristics of Upset Gut Ecology:
- Canker sores
- Stomach aches
- Leg pains
- Sugar Cravings
- Food allergies – especially to dairy
- Bed Wetting
- Nervousness
- Anxiety
- Difficulty falling asleep or staying asleep
- Constipation
- Repeated ear infections
- Thrush, athlete's foot, etc.
- Rashes, eczema
- Night terrors

The good news is that it may be quite simple to get the ecology of your child's gut back into balance – and to greatly reduce or even eliminate the bad effects they are experiencing. Dr. Galland recommends doing this with food; however, Dianne knows that in real life, it can be hard to get these kids to be willing to eat the foods necessary to get their guts back on track.

Because of this, she suggests several supplements which will be easier to get your child to take:

1. Take Probiotics – Plant Acidophilus in your child's gut 3 times a day for 3 months. Dianne recommends exact brands with which she has seen the best results. These probiotics are refrigerated and they are potent!

2. Get Rid of Excess Yeast – Use an antifungal agent such as Grapefruit Seed Extract or Caprylic Acid for 3 months 3 times a day.

3. Reduce sugar or sugary carbs – Try to reduce sugar & carbs by increasing protein, especially at breakfast and snacks. This helps build up the adrenal gland which stabilizes our mood and gives us more energy.

Dianne explains these and several other suggestions as well in her ***Biology of Behavior***[10] audio CDs, which I highly recommend. She also discusses how antibiotics are wonderful, healing medications; however, they do have some harmful side effects. The big problem Dianne talks about is that they upset the ecology of your child's gut.

Both of my sons had multiple ear infections and were on antibiotics quite a bit as babies. Because of this, my husband and I decided to try Dianne's suggestion of the Acidophilus and grapefruit seed extract three times a day. We noticed a difference in our sons within days! We were so pleased that we quickly put our sons on the rest of Dianne's regimen as well.

Over time, we have tweaked what supplements our sons take according to what seems to work best for them. My husband and I have also started taking many of these supplements ourselves. We have noticed such a difference not only in our sons but in us as well.

---

[10] Biology of Behavior by Dianne Craft

Some children may genuinely require medication for their attention and focusing difficulties; however, that isn't always the case. If your child struggles with any of the above symptoms, consider purchasing Dianne's *Biology of Behavior* CDs and listen to what she has to say.

We've been thrilled with the results that we have seen and want to share what we have learned with other families who may be having similar struggles. Listen to what Dianne has to say and see for yourself! It's worth making the effort to try some of these dietary changes and supplements when you know what a positive impact it could have on your child's behavior.

Smart Kids Who Hate to Write

Does your Child Have Dysgraphia?

I've always known that my boys were smart. They started talking before they were one year old. They started learning to read when they were three. They've always been able to come up with intricate stories in their heads, carry on wonderful conversations, think logically, and remember all sorts of facts. The one thing they have always struggled with in our homeschool was that they didn't want to write anything down.

This is a big deal! Writing is one of those skills that you use in all of your subjects. We typically teach spelling by having kids write their words several times. We teach lots of subjects by having the child fill out a workbook page to see what he remembers. We give tests where kids are asked to write things down. Even notebooking and lapbooking require the child to write out what he remembers about certain subjects.

My boys could talk to you endlessly about what they remembered – but as soon as I would ask them to write anything down, they would freeze up and balk at having to write a short sentence or two.

I've asked people for advice over the years and have been given different tips. When my boys were younger, people told me they might not be mature enough to write, yet. I was told to give them time and let them complete most of their work orally.

As they got older and I got more concerned, I was given lots of advice such as:
- Give them more practice
- Buy them another handwriting curriculum
- Continue to work with them
- Build up their hand muscles
- Work on their fine motor skills

I tried everything and they did make some strides in this area; but, it was still a lot of effort whenever they had to write anything down. I quickly learned ways to adapt our curriculum so that my boys would still learn things without having to produce as much written work.

My boys were learning – but something just didn't feel right to me. I couldn't understand why they had to work so hard to write anything down? Was it laziness? Was it a character issue? Would they ever grow out of this?

Fortunately, when my boys were in their tween years, my questions were finally answered. While attending our state's homeschool convention, I had the opportunity to attend six workshops taught by an amazing woman named Dianne Craft.

She has a master's degree in special education, she's a certified nutritional health professional, and she was a homeschool mom.

She taught several workshops that weekend; but, the first one that caught my eye was called **Smart Kids Who Hate to Write**. I knew I needed to attend that workshop. I was just hoping that I might learn one or two things that could give my boys some relief in this area. I believe that what I discovered will change their lives!

Dianne said that writing is an activity in which we should be using both hemispheres of our brain. Once we learn how to do something, after 6 months it is supposed to transfer over to the automatic processing part of our brain. If children are struggling to write, often it is because this doesn't happen. For these kids, they continue having to think about the letters they're forming and the words they're writing instead of that becoming an automatic process.

Dianne gave the analogy of learning to drive a car. She reminded us of what a difficult task this first was when we started to learn. We had to think about where our feet should be and how to push the different pedals. We had to think about when to use our turn signals and which lane to drive in. We had to remember to check behind, around, and in front of us before changing lanes. There were so many different things to think about that we had to use all of our focus to drive. We couldn't talk at the same time and it wasn't enjoyable. In fact, it was quite stressful.

Driving remained difficult for us until we had practiced long enough that the various processes necessary for us to drive transferred over into our automatic hemisphere. Then driving became enjoyable. We could carry on a conversation while driving. We could sing with the radio. It was a whole different ballgame. We could turn our head to look at the sights. It became a much more relaxing experience!

This is what some of our kids feel like when they are writing. Instead of being able to write and think about anything else at the same time, they have to focus hard just to write anything down. This takes a tremendous amount of energy and focus and having to write anything down zaps much of their strength.

Sometimes this problem is caused by your child having a mixed dominance. Normally, if your child is right handed his right eye will be dominant. And if he is left handed his left eye will be dominant.

For some kids, this isn't the case. One of my sons is left handed but his right eye is dominant. This can cause confusion in the brain while he is writing and can cause the writing process to be stopped from entering the automatic hemisphere.

Sometimes a child's brain is hardwired for left handedness even though he is right handed or vice versa. This can also cause major stress in his writing system.

How can you tell if there is stress in your child's writing system?
- If he hates to write – or takes a long time to do so
- If he has a mixed dominance
- If he occasionally reverses his letters or numbers after age 7

- If he is right handed but he makes the letter 'O' clockwise
- If he forms some letters from bottom to top
- If his copy work takes a long time and is labor intensive
- If he does his math problems in his head to avoid writing them down
- If his writing looks sloppy
- If he tell great stories orally but writes very little down
- If he has a hard time lining up his math problems
- If he presses hard when writing
- If he is a teenager but he avoids writing at all costs
- If he mixes his capital and small letters when writing

If your child is exhibiting even one or two of these symptoms then he would benefit from going through Dianne's **Brain Integration Therapy**[11]. This sounds complicated but it's actually simple and inexpensive and it's something you can do at home with your child.

This therapy was initially developed by Dr. Geteman and Dr. Paul Dennison. These exercises not only help your child to overcome his dysgraphia but they will also improve his hand-eye coordination and his awareness of his body in space. They will help him to perform better in sports as well as to write with ease.

The **Brain Integration Therapy** is simple yet it involves lots of steps. I can't detail how to do them in this book because I don't want to take the chance of missing a step and making you waste your time. I would recommend, instead, that you purchase the following products by Dianne Craft:

---

[11] Brain Integration Therapy by Dianne Craft

- ***Brain Integration Therapy Manual***

- ***Smart Kids Who Hate to Write***[12] ***(DVD)***

I purchased these products myself and have been thrilled with what I have discovered so far. Her ***Brain Integration Therapy Manual*** is easy to understand and easy to follow. The ***Smart Kids Who Hate to Write*** DVD includes the entire workshop that I attended and explains the reasoning behind this therapy.

It also includes examples of kids who are a variety of ages doing the writing eight exercise, which is the main therapy that she recommends for overcoming dysgraphia. There are so many other exercises which are beneficial in her brain training manual, however, that I would HIGHLY recommend you purchase that as well.

> *Dianne said that in her over 30 years of teaching this to children she has never met a child she wasn't able to help.*

If your child is struggling to write, purchasing these items will be a small price to pay to see his suffering end in this area. I can't tell you how relieved I am! My boys are also excited to start this therapy.

Dianne says that your child might consider these exercises boring and that's true. When we first started the exercises, however, my boys were thrilled that they might be able to overcome something which has been causing them grief for

---

[12] Smart Kids Who Hate to Write by Dianne Craft

many years. **My only regret is that I didn't hear about this earlier so they wouldn't have had to suffer for so long.**

Dianne says that you will start to see results after a few months; but, that you need to do the therapy for 6 months to a year so that the brain is permanently trained. Dianne said that in her over 30 years of teaching this to children she has never met a child she wasn't able to help.

My boys both did all of Dianne's brain training for about seven months and it did help them. Writing is still not their favorite thing in the world to do – but they are no longer reversing letters, writing from bottom to top, stuff like that.

I do allow them to choose between typing and writing their assignments for most things. They used to try to do all of their math in their head so they wouldn't have to write anything down; but, now they're able to write it out on paper. I think the exercises also helped my oldest son with his balance and coordination. It was worth the time!

Do yourself and your children a favor. Get Dianne's material. Read some of the articles on her website. Check out her sample audio and video files. I think you'll be as happy as I am that you took the time to make writing easier for your children.

Yes, Your Child Will Learn to Read

If you are a beginning homeschool parent, you are probably eager to get started. You see how much your children enjoy learning and savor watching the light bulb moments as your kids grasp new concepts. If you are homeschooling your kids from the beginning, however, there is one common fear which grips many of our hearts: "Will I be able to teach my child to read?"

I have to admit – I also struggled with this fear. We began homeschooling my oldest son when he was 2 years old! We were living in a large city at the time and my husband and I knew there was no way we would feel comfortable sending our children to the public school there. We decided to try teaching our son preschool level material to basically dip our toes into the waters of homeschooling. We didn't want to commit to something we weren't sure we could successfully accomplish.

The preschool years were filled with many happy memories. We had so much fun with all of the hands-on activities. School was fun! My oldest son enthusiastically clung to learning and teaching was a joy. We felt confident moving forward and committed to homeschooling our sons through the school-aged years.

As our oldest son entered his kindergarten and first grade years, however, the schoolwork started to change. In addition to hands-on activities, there were an increasing number of papers to fill out. And we also started the process of teaching our son to read.

I remember how terrified I was that I would "mess him up" by not teaching him correctly. I asked many veteran homeschool moms the question, "What if he never learns to read?"
I remember them all smiling at me and telling me that he would learn… but that was still my biggest fear. I knew how important reading was to everything else in our children's education and I didn't want to blow it.

Fortunately, reading came naturally to our first son. We went through various phonics programs and within a short period of time, he was reading and reading well. He sped through the different levels of reading books and by the time he was in 2nd grade, he was reading **The Chronicles of Narnia**. Pshew, I had done it. I had taught my son to read. My confidence soared!

When our second son got to the age where we were teaching him to read, however, he didn't take to reading anywhere near as well as our first son had. In fact, he seemed to struggle with reading. We used some of the same phonics programs with him – and branched off to try different programs as well – but he just wasn't progressing at the rate I thought he should.

I used to listen to him read aloud **Amelia Bedelia** and **Mr. Putter and Tabby** level books for what seemed like forever. This son had a hard time keeping his place in the book, so I would use my finger to point to each word until he was able to sound it out properly.

I remember going to the library and searching frantically through the shelves for MORE books which were at the level my son could handle. It was a frustrating time. I racked my brain trying to figure out why this son was struggling so hard when my first son had breezed through the entire process.

Reading continued to be a struggle for this son until he got about halfway through his third grade year. He was having a difficult time transitioning from **Henry and Mudge** type readers to chapter books such as **The Magic Treehouse** series.

> *I racked my brain trying to figure out why this son was struggling so hard when my first son had breezed through the entire process.*

Then, all of a sudden, something clicked inside his brain. After having resisted reading any type of chapter book for several weeks, he suddenly flew through **The Magic Treehouse** books. We haven't looked back since.

In the second half of his 3rd grade year, he read more than 120 books on his own. These were various books such as biographies from the **Childhood of Famous Americans** series all the way up to Young Adult books like the **Redwall** series by Brian Jacques. It was such a giant leap forward for him, after having struggled for so long, that I still shake my head in amazement when I think about it.

Here are some lessons I learned from going through all of this:

- **Kids learn at different paces.** Just because they grow up in the same home and have the same parents, they are not the same. They will learn at different rates. Don't push your children too hard. When they are ready, they will leap forward and surprise you with how quickly they catch up.

- **Kids learn in different ways.** Relax and continue to try different methods with each child until you find one which works for him. Just because something worked for their older siblings doesn't mean it will work for him. Sell the old stuff on Ebay and move on.

- **Don't panic.** The more pressure you put on your child to perform, the longer the process may take. Try to be calm and patient and the process will be more enjoyable for both you and your child.

- **Don't move forward too quickly.** Sometimes you need to stay at the same level or even move backwards a little in order to build up your child's confidence. If you find your child is struggling, go back to books which he can easily read. Let him stay there for awhile before you try pressing ahead again. That may be just what your child needs in order to move forward later.

Yes, your child will learn how to read. People used to teach their children to read by using the only book they had in the house – a King James Bible. With all of the various phonics programs on the market today, there is something out there which will work for your child!

If you have questions, ask. There are plenty of veteran homeschool parents who would love to answer your questions. Don't ever feel like you are the only one facing a certain situation. Don't be embarrassed. We need to be willing to be honest with each other and help each other out when things don't seem to be going as they should.

By the time my second was about to enter 5th grade he was a voracious reader. All that time that I worried about his reading skills, I was putting myself and my son under unnecessary stress.

Your child will learn to read, or compute math problems, or spell or whatever other skill with which your child may struggle. Take a deep breath and press on. Someday you will be amazed at your child's progress as well.

How Much Media Should We Allow into our Homeschools?

The majority of children today spend countless hours watching TV, surfing the internet, playing video games, looking at their cell phones... and the list goes on and on. Media can be an addictive beast which gets hold of the minds of our children and doesn't let go. Because of this, some parents have chosen to completely eliminate all media from their homes.

Is it possible to tame this beast and allow media into our homes? I believe that it is. How much media should we allow into our homeschools? There are actually some great uses for media in our homeschools; however, it does take parental involvement and limits to use it successfully.

Here are some ideas for limiting media:

1. **Curriculum** – More and more publishers are offering their material in the form of computer programs. Some parents choose to have their children learn math or other high-level subjects with which they feel less comfortable in this way. Computer and

online classes are some of the easiest ways to teach a subject with which we are unfamiliar. Foreign languages are a popular subject to learn on the computer. Typing is another subject which children usually learn on the computer.

Some parents teach most of the subjects in a traditional way but reserve one with which their child is struggling to learn on the computer. Computer-based classes also come in handy for parents who are teaching several children of multiple age ranges.

2. Enrichment – Adding a video from the library or an internet video clip to whatever subject you're studying can add some visual interest and excitement to your lessons. We have also found that using pictures, stories, and other tidbits we find on the internet adds another dimension to our study.

Use the internet with caution, however. I always prescreen videos, pictures, and information gathered there. It's important to do this with everything – even materials gathered from the library. There are more and more offensive materials created daily and it is our job to be sure what we are teaching to our children agrees with our worldview.

3. Incentive – When our boys were around the age of 10, we finally broke down and allowed the grandparents to buy them a Wii for Christmas. We had been opposed to video games in our home previously, choosing learning computer games over video games. What caused us to change our minds was the fact that playing the Wii can be physical where playing computer games is not.

The Wii is a great motivator. Our boys have to read books for a certain amount of time each day in order to earn Wii time. They also have to do their schoolwork with a good attitude and complete their chores. We have found that simply threatening to take away Wii time is usually enough to curb whatever negative behavior we are experiencing with our sons.

One caution, however, is that the Wii is highly addictive – for parents as well. Be sure to set a timer when letting your children play and set strict limits on its usage. With these safeguards in place, we have found that it can hold a proper place in our homes.

It is possible to keep media out of our homes… and some families choose to take this route. However, in today's modern society, there is merit to helping our kids learn how to tame the beast before they leave our homes. It can also be beneficial for them to become computer saavy so that they will have those skills to apply to their job someday.

There is no right or wrong answer on this one. You will need to decide how much media to allow in your home. Hopefully after reading this chapter, that decision will be a little bit easier for you to make.

13 Easy Ways to Fit Exercise into your Day

Boys need to move almost as much as they need to breathe. Moving helps their brains to work better. They need to wiggle, fidget, and squirm. Instead of fighting this natural tendency, we should work with it by giving our boys opportunities to move throughout the day!

We all know how important it is to be physically active. The Centers for Disease Control and Prevention recommend that kids get a minimum of 60 minutes of physical activity per day. You might think it will be hard to try to jam another hour of something into your child's day; however, it isn't as difficult to fit exercise into your day as you might think!

Here are 13 Easy Ways to Fit Exercise Into Your Day:

Before Schoolwork Starts

1. **Calisthenics** – Have your children do some light calisthenics before sitting down to do their book work. My boys enjoy competing to see who can do the most push-ups and/or pull-ups. When they first started, neither one of them could do ONE full

push-up correctly. Now, they can drop and give me TWENTY (or more) without a problem.

2. Walk/Run – Go for a walk with your child before you start your lessons for the day. You can also just ask your child to run laps around the house before you get started.

3. Play – Quite often, when kids are playing they are getting exercise. Try sending them outside to jump on the trampoline or ride their bike before you start their daily lessons.
During Schoolwork

4. Breaks – Try to take physical breaks between subjects. Give your child 15 minutes to get the wiggles out before starting a new subject.

5. Phys Ed – Schedule a certain amount of physical education time and allow your child to choose when he does it. I've found that my boys will often choose to start their day with Phys Ed. It's a great way to help them wake up in the morning.

6. Unexpected – Surprise your kids by stopping whatever you're doing and telling them to drop and give you 20. Or suddenly ask them to run down the hall and back 10 times. This is great to do with kids who are reluctant to exercise. The surprise makes it more fun to get some movement in.

7. Incorporate into Lessons – Plan physical activities as part of your lesson (i.e., acting out whatever lesson you just learned, throwing a ball back and forth while studying spelling words, throwing a bunch of words on the floor and having your child jump to the correct word when you give a definition, etc.)

8. Variation – Try scheduling more physical activities between more sedentary ones. If you have younger children, you will also want to be sure to spend some time working on their fine motor skills and gross motor skills.

After Schoolwork or on Weekends

9. Outside Play – Encourage (or require) your kids to get an hour of outside play time each day.

10. Game Systems – Let them play some of the more physical games on the Wii (or other gaming system) such as Active Life, Wii Fit, or Sports Resort. This way they will get exercise without even realizing it. This is especially good during the middle of winter.

11. Sign them up for a Sport – In many areas there are homeschool leagues which are often more family friendly than the public school options.

12. Get Dad Involved – Ask dad to go into the yard with the kids and toss a football, throw a baseball, shoot some free throws, kick the soccer ball around, etc.

13. Get the Family Involved – Try to do something more physically active as a family. Take a hike, go on a bike ride, go camping, etc.

As you can see, it isn't as hard as you might think to fit exercise into your day. With a little bit of thinking, you can help your child to have the healthy habit of being more active! And the more your son moves the more likely he is to retain the information that he is learning. It's definitely worth the effort.

Turning our Boys into Men

It may be politically incorrect to raise our sons as knights in shining armor – but it is also much appreciated by those surrounding us. Everywhere we go, people quickly notice that my sons are different. They are able to walk quietly through a store with minimum squabbles, they share with each other, they can sit in a restaurant and enjoy a meal with the rest of the family… nothing extraordinary. And yet, in today's world my boys stand out from the pack. They are developing good character and it shows.

It is a common occurrence for people to approach us and tell us what good boys we are raising. How have manners and self-control become so lacking in today's society? Schools have thrown out God, they've thrown out prayer, and they've thrown out right and wrong. Children in public schools are being taught to do what makes them feel good in the context of a world with no absolute truth. Anything goes!

In our world of moral relativism, homeschoolers can be a beacon of light to a dark world. We have the opportunity to spend as much time as we'd like training our children about truth, developing their character, and helping them to be discerning about what's right and what's wrong in our world.

Please remember to take time out from your book lessons to teach your sons those real life lessons which will help them to make good decisions throughout their lives. **You cannot spend too much time developing your son's character!** Remember, these lessons are better caught than taught.

> *In our world of moral relativism, homeschoolers can be a beacon of light to a dark world.*

Show your sons how to make a meal for a hurting neighbor, how to mow an elderly widow's lawn, how to volunteer at church or at a soup kitchen, and how to treat others with respect. If our sons grow up with the golden rule as their guide, they will become men of character who are looked up to by their peers… and men who are able to make a difference in our world.

Check out the below resources for more on this topic:

- *Boyhood and Beyond: Practical Wisdom for Becoming a Man*[13]
- *Created for Work: Practical Insights for Young Men*[14]

---

[13] Boyhood and Beyond by Bob Schultz
[14] Created for Work by Bob Schultz

4 Benefits from Allowing Your Child to Make Mistakes

When our boys are little, we make all of their decisions for them. We give instructions and we expect them to be followed. As boys grow up, however, they begin to have a strong feeling that they should be making some of their own decisions.

Even young sons should be allowed to make some of their own minor decisions. Once our sons are around middle school age, however, it is vital that your son knows you are listening to him and that he has some input.

A great way to show your son respect is to let him make even more of his own decisions. We need to learn when it is appropriate to back off a little bit and allow them more independence. If we don't let our sons make any of their own decisions, they will resist obeying anything that we ask them to do.

We all know that our sons will not always make good decisions. We need to remember that we don't always make good decisions, either.

Here are 4 benefits from allowing your child to make mistakes:

1. **Self-confidence** – Kids develop self confidence when they are allowed to make decisions on their own. Allow them to figure out how to do it rather than always jumping in immediately and showing them how. This also helps them to be brave and not be so afraid of failure that they are reluctant to try new things.

2. **Build coping skills** – Kids develop many important skills in life as they are allowed to go through difficult situations. They learn how to handle negative emotions, build self control, apologize, and many other important relational skills.

> *If we don't let our sons make any of their own decisions, they will resist obeying anything that we ask them to do.*

3. **Learn to take responsibility** – When kids are allowed to make some of their own decisions, they will also have the opportunity to deal with the consequences. Sometimes they will make poor decisions and this will give them practice learning to take responsibility for their actions. Sometimes they will make good decisions and this will help them to feel good about the choices they have made.

4. Developing wisdom – As our kids are allowed to make some decisions on their own, they will learn from the natural consequences of their decisions. This will help them to make wiser decisions in the future. We want them to have the freedom to fail while they are still living under our authority and they aren't making decisions which could affect their entire life negatively.

Some areas where we could relax a bit and let them call the shots are:

- Hairstyle (within reason)
- Clothing (as long as it is modest and within the budget)
- Some school subjects (be sure he's studying some things he enjoys)
- What order he completes his studies (who cares when he does it as long as it gets done?)
- Extracurricular activities (be sure you aren't trying to live vicariously through your child)
- Help decide menu items on certain days (we all like to eat food we think is delicious)

Sometimes kids are hesitant to make certain decisions on their own. Some boys may resist attempting certain tasks which we feel confident they can handle at their age. In these situations, we should gently guide our children to experience some new things to expand their horizons and help them to mature.

Some boys will naturally want to lead and you'll have to try to hold them back. Other boys might be more hesitant and our job is to gently but firmly push them to take the lead role in certain areas. If we allow kids to go through certain experiences when they are living at home, we will have the opportunity to work with them much more closely.

It can be hard for parents to let go and allow their sons to make some of their own decisions. We need to remember, however, that allowing them to make decisions is good training. As we step back and allow them to have some control over their lives, they will learn to be more independent, confident, and responsible.

Not all of the decisions our sons make will be good ones. In these situations, we can work with our boys to help them learn from their mistakes.

> *Not all of the decisions our sons make will be good ones.*

We went through a situation with one of our sons where we let him make a decision even though we felt that he was making a mistake. Our youngest son attended a Homeschool Performing Arts acting camp one summer and he loved it!

After attending the camp, he was super excited to audition for HPA's main production. Unfortunately, we found out that practices for that production took place at the same time as a different opportunity for both our boys for which we had already committed and paid.

Our son had the option of participating in an HPA Kids production instead, which was for 6-12 year olds. He was 12; however, he was so tall that he wanted to act with the older kids that year. He said that he didn't feel like an average 12-year-old because he was so tall. He said that he would rather take the year off of acting and just try out for their production next year instead of acting with kids his own age and younger.

My husband and I felt that he was making a mistake. We encouraged him to try out for HPA Kids. We prayed with him. But he made his decision and we felt that it was time for us to step back and let him experience the consequences.

This was hard for me to do. I wanted to force him to join HPA Kids because I was sure he would love it. But allowing him to choose how he proceeded ultimately taught him more than if we decided for him.

By the way, he did end up taking a different drama class that year and it ended up being a great experience for him!

Consider allowing your son to make some of his own decisions this coming year. We need to allow our boys to experience the natural consequences of their decisions whenever possible. These experiences, good and bad, will help them to mature… and to make even wiser decisions in the future.

5 Ways to Find Out What's in Your Son's Heart

When I was a little girl, I wanted to be a writer. I dreamed about becoming a published author and writing books that would change society as we know it today! Fortunately, I was blessed with my 7th grade English teacher, Mrs. Tittle, who sacrificed many a lunch period to read my stories and give me feedback. Becoming an author was definitely in my heart.

As I grew older and people would ask me what I wanted to be, I began to change my answer. You see, when I told people I wanted to be a writer, they looked amused and/or disappointed because becoming an author isn't something that many people can support themselves with. So over time, I began to stuff down my desire to be a writer and started telling people I wanted to become a lawyer instead.

Now, don't get me wrong. This wasn't anything that was done consciously on my part! But the reaction I got when I told people I wanted to be a lawyer was MUCH MORE POSITIVE than the reaction I got when telling them I wanted to be an author.

So, writer was out and lawyer was in. I thought I wanted to become a lawyer for years and years... until I went off to college. Then, when my dad asked me what I wanted to major in I told him I wanted to be a writer. He said it was fine to study writing but I needed to at least get a minor in something solid that I could fall back on for getting a job. So I majored in writing and minored in computer science.

My first real job after college was as a technical writer; but, after that job fizzled out, I went on to make a good living in the computer industry as a network administrator.

There were times in my twenties when I thought about going back to school to get my law degree. Every time I thought about it, however, I thought about how much money and time I would have to spend going to law school. And I knew that someday if I was blessed enough to get married and have kids I'd want to quit my job and stay home with them. And I wasn't sure I actually wanted to be a lawyer, anyway. So I never pursued that goal.

Was the guidance my dad gave me before college the best advice? It did help me to get a job. But, did it keep me from pursuing what was actually in my heart?

What's in your son's heart?

Fast forward to several years later when I had become a wife and a mom to two tween boys. One night, I had gone upstairs to tuck my sons into bed… Quite often, bedtime is an opportunity to have some nice, heart-to-heart talks with my boys.

During one of these talks, my younger son told me that he wanted to become an actor. This was coming from the son who used to be so shy that he had to whisper his Awana verses into his teacher's ear because of his fear to say them in front of the whole class.

He wanted to be an actor? Not only that, he said that he felt like God wanted him to become a Hollywood actor in blockbuster movies. He said that he felt that he was going to make a lot of money and he was supposed to use that money to help lots and lots of people.

He was extremely emotional as he was talking to me. It was clear that this meant a great deal to him. So I tried to swallow my surprise. I told him I didn't know anything about acting, but we would figure out what he should do and take the first step. The fact that I was open to what he was saying allowed him to feel comfortable talking to me and telling me more of what was on his heart. It was an amazing experience.

I haven't always been the best at hearing what's in my sons' hearts. Unfortunately, there were several times when my other son told me that he'd like to become a professional baseball player or possibly a sports commentator and I wasn't as supportive.

I didn't completely shoot down his ideas – but I remember telling him that there weren't many people who were good enough to become professional ball players... and that sports commentators were usually ex-players... My words weren't supportive. I was unintentionally discouraging his dreams. And I didn't make any effort to try to help him take steps toward those dreams, either.

> *I haven't always been the best at hearing what's in my sons' hearts.*

My younger son is definitely benefiting from some of the prior mistakes I made with his older brother.

There are 5 ways to find out what's in your son's heart:

1. Be in prayer – This is the most important thing you can do for your child. Ask God to tell you what He would have for your son. Ask Him what He wants you to teach him. Ask Him to show you how He wants your son to fit into His big plan. Ask God to help you hear His voice as you're discipling your son.

2. Be willing to listen – You need to listen to your son even if what you're hearing doesn't make sense to you, seems unrealistic, or is downright scary.

3. Be willing to help – Our kids need our help determining a plan of action. What do they need to learn in order to pursue their dreams? What resources exist in your area which could help them? Are there any mentors you could find for them in their area of interest?

4. Be willing to accommodate them – Are there things you could be teaching them as part of their homeschooling which will give them some needed training? Are there ways you could make pursuing their dreams more attainable by being flexible with homeschool hours or subjects? Are you willing to do the driving or the volunteering to help them make their dreams a reality?

5. Be encouraging – If your child has a huge dream, don't feel like you need to poke holes in it so that he will see reality. Help him to go for it. If God has given our child a dream, who are we to say that it isn't possible? With God, everything is possible!

We recently had a situation with our oldest son where he respectfully came to me and said he didn't want to be involved in an activity which we had signed up AND PAID FOR several months prior. He told me his reasons why and we had an excellent discussion about it.

What he was telling me wasn't what I wanted to hear. I felt that this activity would be good for him. And truth be told, I was also looking forward to getting to know the moms at this activity better as well.

However, my husband and I discussed it and we felt that we needed to listen to our son this time. Even though we didn't agree with him, we wanted to show him that we cared about what was in his heart. It was hard for us to give up the money we had already spent, the possibility of relationships with like-minded moms, and the useful skills we thought he would learn… but our relationship with our son was more important than any of those things.

It's definitely possible to find out what's going on in your son's heart and to develop a closer relationship with him. You should be aware that there is often a personal price to pay. We need to let go of our own expectations but it's definitely worth it. I can't tell you how much more willing our son has been to open up to us since we were willing to respect his feelings and listen to what he valued most.

By the way, not too long ago my husband and I were talking about what we had always wanted to be when we were kids and I talked about wanting to be a writer. My husband said, "You do realize that you are a writer now, don't you?!?"

It took a minute for that to sink in. I am a writer. I have realized my childhood dream – no matter how farfetched it had seemed at the time. I guess that just goes to show that childhood dreams can come true – for us as well as for our sons!

Tangible Ways to Express Love to Your Son

Several years ago, I had the opportunity to hear a lecture given by Diana Waring, author of the ***History Revealed***[15] curriculum as well as several helpful books for parents. Diana's talk was extremely convicting for me! She had a fresh perspective on homeschooling that could transform our relationships with our children if we heed her advice.

Diane said that it's easy for us to focus too much on academics and forget about some even more important aspects of training our children. She said that for our homeschooling to be successful, it must be built on a strong foundation which is based on the love we have for our children. We need to remember that love throughout the day and express it to our kids.

Here are 5 tangible ways to express love to your children:

- **Be Loving** – Smile at your children. That sounds pretty basic; however, if we pay attention to our facial expressions,

---

[15] http://www.dianawaring.com/store/history-curriculum

we might be surprised at what we see. It's easy to become so serious that our kids think we are perpetually scowling at them. Be sure your face is giving your children the right message.

- **Be Kind** – There is never an excuse for saying unkind things to our children. No matter how upset we might feel, we need to maintain self control.

- **Be Encouraging** – We need to stop being so uptight about what our kids aren't learning. Every child is different. Some will struggle in areas in which we excel. When we struggle, it feels good to have someone come alongside us and help us to have a break through. We need to do that for our children.

> *It's easy to become so serious that our kids think we are perpetually scowling at them.*

- **Delight in Your Kids** – Do our children see our eyes twinkle when they walk into the room – or do we subtly express irritation at the interruption? Do we show them how in love we are with them? We need to enjoy our children! The time we are given with them is fleeting. Don't waste even a moment of this time by wishing you (or they) were somewhere else.

- **Be Transparent** – We need to let our kids see who we really are. We also need to let our kids be who they really are rather than trying to shape them into some preconceived mold we have in our heads.

Most homeschool parents would agree that teaching our children character is much more important and lasting than is academics. Our homeschools often don't reflect this belief, however.

We spend countless hours on academics, only to be too distracted throughout the day to impart character into our children. Educating our children is only one of the tasks we undertake as parents. We also need to be sure we are parenting them properly, disciplining them, and being caregivers.

Homeschooling gives us the opportunity to learn together, laugh together, work together, serve one another, and walk humbly. Never forget that there is plenty of stuff that we don't know as well. When you learn something new together, don't be afraid to get excited with your children.

It's natural for us to want to protect our children. Sometimes, in an effort to do what's best for them, we can have a tendency to place them in boxes to ensure that their world is small enough and simple enough that they will turn out alright without God's moment-by-moment help.

When this happens, our homes can become legalistic, focus too much on external behavior, and we can tend toward wanting perfection from our children. Boxes are behavior-oriented and are made up of man's rules, man's judgments, and self-righteousness.

How are we able to get rid of these boxes and live a life which will be more likely to pass on our faith, instill character in our children, and build a strong relationship with our children?

Diana reminds us of the following timeless truths:

- We need to remember that love is messy and doesn't always follow the rules.

- We need to love our children unconditionally and not just when they perform.

- We need to give our children dignity and respect. If we want it from them, we need to model it by giving it to them first.

- We need to have compassion on our children. Learning can be hard work! We need to stop being drill sergeants and start being loving teachers.

- We need to be humble and not think that we always know more (or better) than do our children.

In this way, we can teach our children the academics while also teaching them what it means to be a valuable member of our family. We can train them to have good character while we show them what it feels like to be loved unconditionally. Once we've won our child's heart, teaching the academics will fall into place.

Do Your Words Inspire or Demoralize Your Children?

We've gone through some good years of homeschooling and some bad ones. As my boys have matured, it has been wonderful to watch as they have breakthroughs in certain areas.

For instance, one son, who always used to feel like his arm would break if he had to write anything down, suddenly started to write novels. The other son, who would get so frustrated with math that he would often break down in tears while trying to complete a simple problem, suddenly found a curriculum he clicked with and math became one of his favorite subjects.

As homeschool moms it's important for us to continually try to reevaluate and determine what is working, what isn't working, or what could be better. One Sunday as our pastor was preaching about taming the tongue, I felt like I'd been hit by a ton of bricks. The entire sermon was convicting; however, the statement that transformed our homeschool as well as our family life was this:

"Are your children inspired or demoralized by your words?"

Whoa. Are my children inspired by my words? Not do they obey my words, do they listen to my words, do they understand my words… but are they inspired by them. Wow, that statement hit me like a ton of bricks.

To my shame, at the time that I heard this, I hadn't thought about inspiring my boys by my words in a long time. Maybe not ever. I thought of inspiring them, of course. I would research for hours to find the best curriculum for them. I poured over resources to determine the best books to inspire their minds. I knew how powerful words could be. But MY words? I definitely didn't give them as much thought as I should have.

Obviously, homeschooled kids spend an inordinate amount of time with the parent who is teaching them – usually their mom. And homeschool moms are notoriously busy. Not only do we have to run a household but we also have to teach our children of various ages at the same time.

At times, it can be a stressful process. We don't get many moments to ourselves… and quite often when we are just about to get a few minutes to work on something we'd like to do, one of our children inevitably comes up and needs our attention.

In that split second, we have a choice. We can either talk to our child in a kind, patient way or we can answer him with frustration in our voice. That type of tone can be demoralizing to our children. Do we want them to feel that we are there for them whenever they need us? Or do we want them to feel that they are a burden to us? Or that a clean house is more important than they are?

Even more than this, are we speaking in a way that is actually inspiring to our children? Do we ask them to do things in a lackluster manner or do we phrase things in such a way that they actually want to do them? Do we ignite their individual passions? Do we engage them with the material we are presenting?

> *Do we want them to feel that we are there for them whenever they need us? Or do we want them to feel that they are a burden to us?*

This is true whether we are teaching a subject or simply trying to maintain order in the house. After hearing that sermon, I decided to test out that theory. I have told my sons hundreds of times that when they come inside they need to neatly put their shoes on their designated shoe rack – not just to kick them off anywhere on the floor and race inside.

When I walked into our mud room that day, I saw shoes scattered all over the floor. Not only that, the mudroom bench was full of various backpacks, books, and other paraphernalia that had been tossed there as my eager boys entered the house.

I instantly felt my blood pressure rise as thoughts of, "How many times do I have to tell these boys…" raced through my head. As I whirled around to find my sons, I realized that the next words to leave my mouth could be inspiring or demoralizing. What was I going to choose?

As I neared my sons, I decided to try the inspiring route. Instead of chastising them yet again, I changed my tone to one of eagerness and excitement and said, "Hey, guys, Dad's going to be home, soon. Can you imagine how excited he would be if he came inside and the mud room was spotless?!? Why don't you go clean up your stuff real quick. Then we can watch when he comes inside and see his reaction. I bet he'll be amazed!"

My boys looked at me in surprise. Then they looked at each other. It took them about 5 seconds before they leapt up and raced to the mud room. I watched in disbelief as they cleaned that mud room until it was spic and span. No more direction was needed from me. They did a spectacular job and they did it with excitement.

That was a huge lesson for me. Our boys are waiting to be inspired. Sure, there are plenty of times that we can get after them. They all have areas in which they struggle - just as we do. However, if you take the time to approach your sons with encouragement versus discouragement, you will all come away from the experience with a better attitude.

This is also important to remember when we are teaching our children – especially if it is a subject we dislike or with which we struggle. The way we approach the material will either light a passion in our children or it will also cause them to dislike the material.

For example, history can be seen as dry, boring and irrelevant – or it can be an exciting adventure filled with emotional stories of real people who struggled just as we do. We need to give our children every chance to feel passionate about learning.

There are many things in life that we can't control. However, we are in complete control of what we say and how we say it. We need to remember what a powerful influence we have over our children.

Do our words inspire them?

I made a vow that year that I would be more mindful of the words I spoke. More than any curriculum change, any books read, or any field trips taken I believe this has had an even greater impact on my boys. I challenge us all to ponder the impact of our words BEFORE we say them.

Conformed or Transformed?

I recently went to a homeschool convention where I heard an amazing speaker named Steve Demme[16], the creator of Math-U-See. Steve has been a pastor, a Christian school teacher, and a homeschool dad. The premise of one of Steve's lectures was that we need to remember why we are home educating our children.

Steve talked about why public schools were started in the first place. Schools met for a short time of the year, between the harvest and winter time, when the snows would cause children to stay home. These parents sent their children to school to learn how to read the Bible and to learn how to use math in daily life.

Steve's point was that sometimes homeschooling parents feel pressured to give their children a "better" education than what they would have received in school. In this quest, we can become obsessed with filling our child's day with more and more schoolwork until they break under the pressure. This is unnecessary and sad for the children.

---

[16] http://www.buildingfaithfamilies.org/.

We shouldn't have an assembly line mentality about our child's education. Their day should not be filled with worksheet after worksheet. We need to be focusing more on living out the word of God in front of our children so that they can catch the most important lessons of life.

Our main goals for home education should be training our kids for eternity. This means focusing on their character and not just their grades. Homeschoolers are together all day long in close quarters giving them the opportunity to learn how to get along with others in this setting. We also have more time to spend with our children teaching them to start each day out with devotions, managing household responsibilities, and learning to help parents and siblings throughout the day.

> **We need to be sure we don't conform to the pressure to do these same things to our children.**

Many kids in public school have days filled with schoolwork and nights filled with homework. They also have extracurricular activities which fill up any free time they may have otherwise had. They don't have time to spend their daily time with God, read a book for pleasure, play a board game with the family, go on a leisurely walk in the woods, or play with their siblings.

Are our homes conformed to the pattern of public schools or are they transformed? As homeschoolers, we need to be sure we don't conform to the pressure to do these same things to our children. We must be careful not to fill up our child's day to the point where they don't have time for the important things in life.

5 Vital Things You Can Do to "Harden Off" Your Son

Our family usually has quite a large garden in the summer. We love to plant all sorts of various fruits and vegetables. It's much easier to buy transplanted plants to stick right into the garden than it is to buy seeds. However, these plants cost a lot. So we usually buy seeds for whatever can be stuck directly into the ground and we buy transplants for other things such as herbs, peppers, and tomatoes.

One year, however, I decided I wanted to try growing my herbs, peppers, and tomatoes from seed. I did a ton of research, bought seed mats and grow lights, and got to work. In our area, seeds need to be started indoors in March. So, I carefully watered my seeds and watched them grow. I was so careful with my little seedlings. I did everything in my power that I knew to do to help them grow into healthy plants.

After several months of growing these seeds under ideal conditions, it was time for me to take my plants outside. I knew my plants needed to be "hardened off" before they could survive outside. That basically means that the plants need to be slowly introduced to the more harsh reality of the outdoor weather so that their chance of survival increases.

So, I stuck my plants in my wheelbarrow and wheeled them out into the shade for a few hours. At night, I wheeled them back into the garage. I did this for several days.

Finally, we had a beautiful, sunny day. I wheeled my plants out into the sun and let them stay there for the afternoon. When I came back, my plants were completely wilted and even looked burnt. I had spent months and months of babying my plants only to scorch them in the span of a few hours. Talk about heartbreaking!

We need to be sure we don't do this same thing to our boys. In my opinion, boys in school are exposed to things before they are ready. They are forced to leave their homes and be responsible for themselves in a way that my boys never had to at those young ages. School kids grow up so much earlier than do homeschooled kids – and I think that it is hard on them in a way that is completely unnecessary.

On the other hand, at some point we do need to expose our homeschooled boys to certain things so that they won't be completely shocked once they leave our homes. It's a "hardening off" approach which is so necessary to ensure our boys will survive the transition from the safety of our homes to the harsh reality of the world.

Here are 5 Vital Things You Can Do to "Harden Off" Your Son:

1. **Get him an outside coach or mentor** – My boys have enjoyed participating in a competitive basketball league, through the years, and it has helped to mature them greatly.

When they were younger, they played on more recreational sports teams; however, most of these teams were led by fathers who were coerced into the job. My boys did learn lots of things from the more casual leagues. They learned good sportsmanship, being part of a team, and the mechanics of the game. But, being part of a competitive league took them to a whole new level.

Their coach pushed them a lot harder physically than they had ever been pushed before. My boys came out of those practices with ashen faces and dripping sweat. They collapsed in their beds after they got home. Their coach got them to give their all.

If I had tried to get my boys to work that hard, they would have insisted that they were tired. They rose to the challenge when their coach demanded that kind of effort. Having a coach helped them to get stronger and to learn more quickly than if either myself or my husband were the ones encouraging/pushing them.

2. **Let Dad decide** – Our husbands have a better idea of when our son's playing, behavior, and joking are appropriate than do us moms. When I hear my boys using mild bathroom humor it isn't funny to me. I have visions of them growing up to be rude, crude men. I hear my boys wrestling or arguing back and forth and I'm afraid that someone is going to get hurt. My husband has

to tell me when they're just joking around or they're both having fun. I have a hard time seeing it.

> *Our husbands have a better idea of when our son's playing, behavior, and joking are appropriate than do us moms.*

Here's a little secret you might not realize: Guys don't act the same around us women as they do when they're in an all male environment. My husband often goes to Men's Retreats with a bunch of guys from our conservative church. He has told me just a few things that go on at these retreats – and even pastors are involved (gasp!) There are practical jokes; loud, competitive body functions; and other raucous behavior.

Guys like to let their hair down when they're away from us women. It's normal for your son to be gross on occasion. You can, however, teach your son that there is a time and a place. My husband is training our boys not to act like that when a lady is present. Or, at least, that's what he's trying to do. We aren't quite there yet.

3. Youth Group – There are different opinions in the homeschool community about whether or not we should allow our kids to be involved in youth group. I don't always agree with everything that goes on in our youth group; but, I do think it has been a good experience for my boys. They have had a chance to gain some independence from our family at these events. They've had a chance to put their faith in action while they're still at home to discuss hard situations and to get advice from mom and dad.

I know that our youth group also has a heart for helping kids to own their faith. And they are teaching the kids to have a servant's heart. Every year, they participate in an event called "A Widow Bit of Help" where they help the widows in our church with yard work. Once a month, the youth group puts on a church service for a nursing home in our area. My boys have enjoyed these service opportunities as much as they've appreciated the events which are merely entertaining and fellowship building.

Being part of this group is also helping them to see other adults who are putting their faith into action. It helps them to see that Mom and Dad aren't the only Christians who believe "this stuff." Some cool people actually believe it, too! ☺

4. Some Cyber Experience – My boys enjoy playing Minecraft. They love meeting on a server with one of their cousins and building extremely complicated bases together. Recently, they had spent a bunch of time creating a detailed base… when some bully with diamond armor came along and killed them all. He took over their base and they had to start over.

My Mommy Heart was broken. I didn't know how someone could do something so mean! I was about to say that we needed to find a different server for them where there weren't any bullies when my boys came out of our office laughing and with adrenaline pumping. They had had a meeting to determine how they could come up with better strategies so that they wouldn't be so easily defeated next time. They were energized by the experience!

Our world is not filled with a bunch of nice people. Our kids are going to encounter individuals who don't always treat them with loving kindness. It's good for our boys to have a chance to have some of these experiences now so that they won't be completely shocked when they have a less than supportive boss or an irritating coworker. They need to know how to cope in these difficult situations.

> *Our world is not filled with a bunch of nice people.*

While on the internet, obviously precautions need to be taken. But we live in a technological world and our boys will benefit from feeling comfortable with technology and knowing how to wield it in a good way.

5. In Over Their Head – People used to teach their kids how to swim by throwing them into a lake and letting them save themselves. While I don't necessarily advocate that type of behavior, I do think it's good to sometimes put our sons in positions where they feel a little bit out of their league.

Once, my sons' JV basketball coach scheduled a scrimmage against a college basketball team. These guys were saavy basketball players who had obviously been playing together for years. They made numerous 3 point shots. If you could get 4 pointers, some of them would have made those as well. They were passing halfway across the court, they dunked the ball, they stole the ball from our guys like crazy, and they won... 108-8.

It was crazy watching this game as a mom. I wanted to walk up to one of the college guys later and say, "Are you proud of yourself for dunking the ball while being guarded by my 12 year old?!?"

> *Being on the losing end of a landslide game had helped them to overcome their fears.*

But the reaction my boys game me after the game shocked me. My oldest son said, "I was really nervous for our first game but I'm not anymore." Apparently, they knew they had seen the worst that they could possibly see and they still had fun. They felt more prepared for whatever they would actually encounter during a game. Being on the losing end of a landslide game had helped them to overcome their fears. It wasn't as bad as whatever they were imagining in their heads!

Have you hardened off your son? Do you think he will completely wilt and burn up once he leaves your home or will be ready to flourish in the harsh world in which we find ourselves?

Consider allowing your son to experience some "hardening off" opportunities so that he will be well prepared for whatever he encounters once he is a man living on his own.

"I'm Never Going to Use This!"

10 Things Boys Learn from School Work that they WILL Use

Have you ever heard your son object to doing his school work by saying, "I'm never going to use this!" My boys say this on those days when they would like to do anything other than their school work. I hear this much more often that I would care to admit!

This is a hard objection to respond to because there is some truth to what they are saying. Will they ever need to know the atomic number of various elements later in life? Will they need to be able to complete calculus problems after they're done with school? Will they need to know the difference between a gerund and a present participle – or know how to diagram a sentence? Most of them won't.

So, how do we answer our sons when they ask us this question? Is school a complete waste of time?

Here are 10 things your son will learn from school that he WILL use later in life:

1. Benefits of Memorizing – Our brains are muscles and they must be exercised. Memorizing information is like mental calisthenics. When we train our brains by memorizing information, we give it the strength to retain and remember other information later on.

By the way, it's more beneficial to memorize information over time than it is to cram. Studying information half an hour a day for a week is much more effective than studying for four hours in one sitting.

2. Brainstorming – Our boys need to be able to think outside of the box. They need practice brainstorming both on their own as well as in groups. Give them the time and freedom to be able to brainstorm solutions to various problems throughout their school year.

3. Certain Information WILL be Used Later – Some of the information our sons learn during school will be used on a regular basis. Knowing how to read is essential to success in our daily lives. It's important that our children know enough about history that they aren't doomed to repeat it. Basic math skills are used quite often in regular life. The ability to think logically is vitally important in a society where untruths and propaganda are constantly bombarding us.

Depending on what type of career your child ends up undertaking as an adult, this will be true of other subjects as well. And since you might be unsure of what career your son will pursue at this time in his life, it's important to study a wide range of subjects while he is school aged.

4. Following Directions – When your boss gives you directions, he wants you to follow them completely. He won't give multiple reminders. He won't want to have to hold our boys' hand. Our sons need to be able to receive directions, process them, and complete what they have been asked to do.

5. Getting Along with Others – This skill is priceless in the workforce. Your son will need to be able to get along with his coworkers, his boss, and especially with customers. Difficult customers are some of the hardest people in life to get along with. How better to train for this task than to have to get along with your siblings all day long?

6. How to Learn/Research – Learning how to learn is essential. Throughout our lives, we will need to be able to learn new information. If we don't know how to do something we need to be able to figure out how we can acquire that information – and then learn it.

I am a book lover – but I have to say that the internet has transformed this task for us. It's so easy to watch a You Tube video showing us how to complete a home repair – or pretty much anything else for that matter. It's also wonderful to be able to Google anything that we don't know or understand. There are good and bad aspects to our technological world; but, the ease of researching is definitely one of the good parts.

7. Project Planning – We need to be able to give our sons complex projects and have them handle them from beginning to end. They need to be able to plan ahead, organize their materials, obtain necessary resources, and manage their time. Try starting with small projects and working your way up to more and more complex ones. This is excellent real life practice for them.

8. Respecting Authority – It's important for our boys to respect authority. Whether it's a police officer, a church elder, or a boss, he will need to show proper deference to those in authority over him. He practices this on a regular basis by giving respect to Mom and Dad.

9. Technology – We live in a technological world and our boys need to feel comfortable working with computers. The more familiar your child is with a variety of computer programs, the easier it will be for him to learn additional programs in the future.

There are lots of ways that we've tried to help our boys become familiar with technology. They have both been given digital cameras of their own to use for taking pictures as well as videos. We've allowed them to use computer programs such as Camtasia and Pinnacle Studio to edit their movies. We ask them to type some of their papers in Microsoft Word so that they will know how to use word processing software. When we've had to have additional memory installed, we've allowed our sons to do the installing. We want our boys to feel comfortable sitting down at a computer and figuring stuff out!

10. Time Management – When your boss gives you an assignment with a due date, he will expect you to return to his office with your completed work either by or before the deadline. He will not give constant reminders. Our boys need to learn how to turn in their completed assignments on time as well.

Once our boys leave our homes, we want to be sure that they're equipped to be responsible leaders. The time that we spend teaching them is valuable. We are training their brains to learn and giving them a skill set which will hopefully serve them well in their future careers.

The next time your son complains that he'll never use whatever you're teaching him, have a discussion with him about what he will use. Boys are much more willing to learn when they see the value in what we're teaching them.

Increase their Attention Span

As a general rule, the attention span of boys tends to be shorter than that of girls. Obviously this varies with each child; however, there are more boys who suffer from ADHD. And even boys who have wonderful powers of focus still have a tendency to move, bounce, fiddle with objects, look around, and want to be on the move.

Fortunately, it is possible to promote a healthy environment for your boys which will be more conducive for their homeschooling.

Consider these lifestyle choices to increase the attention span of boys:

- **Organize your day** – A consistent routine is good for all children and especially for boys and/or those who might struggle with ADHD.

- **Turn off the TV** – Keep TV watching and listening to the radio to a minimum. Most children need quiet time without background noise to think, listen, and read to their full potential.

- **Consistent Bedtimes** – Set an early bedtime which will allow your child to get plenty of sleep. If your child is getting 8 hours of sleep per night or less, they are NOT getting adequate rest at night. Children need a surprising amount of sleep – probably more than you think! See the following chart to determine what time your son should be getting to bed each night for optimum performance.

Age	Hours required
5 years	11 hours
6 years	10.75 hours
7 years	10.5 hours
8 years	10.25 hours
9 years	10 hours
10 years	9.75 hours
11 years	9.5 hours
12 years	9.25 hours
13 years	9.25 hours
14 years	9 hours
15 years	8.75 hours
16 years	8.5 hours
17 years	8.25 hours
18 years	8.25 hours

NOTE: Some experts say that kids need even more sleep than this!

- **Breakfast** – Make sure your child has a hearty breakfast with plenty of protein and a multi-vitamin. Having a well-balanced breakfast will help him to think more clearly and not get as tired during his studies.

- **Discipline** – Provide consistent discipline for your children. Set a few clear rules and stick to them. If your sons are well disciplined during regular life, they will also be much better disciplined during school hours.

Your son's attention span should be at least 3-5 minutes long for each year of his age. So, the typical kindergartener should be able to stay on task for at least 15 minutes. When we are homeschooling boys, there are several things we can do to help increase the attention span of boys as well as their enjoyment for learning:

- **Breaks** – Take a break between topics and allow your boys to get up, stretch, run down the hall, or run a few laps around the house. Including some activities for boys such as these will allow them to release their pent up energy and will go a long way towards helping them to stay focused while they study.

- **Change it up** – Boys become bored with the same information or the same methods. If they understand a topic, move on. You can go back and review later to make sure that they fully grasp the information. If you review over and over with boys their minds will disengage. Also, try new techniques with boys. If you usually do math worksheets, try having them answer orally or on the computer. This will help them to remain interested and will increase their attention span.

- **Control** – Boys love to feel that they have at least some control over their studies. Give your sons several choices that you would be happy with and let them make some of the decisions. Or let them decide which subject they are going to tackle next. When boys are given this kind of freedom, you will find yourself struggling with them less throughout the day.

- **Interest Area** – The greatest motivator for boys is to teach them something that interests them. Let your boys pick topics they are interested in and then allow them to explore them fully. They can do this in addition to their regular studies or during breaks. Their excitement for all of their studies will increase when you allow them to pursue things they love as well what you want them to study.

- **Manipulatives** – Give your boys objects that they can taste, touch, smell and see. Boys learn well with tactile, kinesthetic learning. The more of their senses you can incorporate into their activities, the more understanding and enjoyment they will have of their lessons.

- **Movement** – Provide plenty of opportunities for movement. Boys have lots of energy. If you allow them to expend this energy in accepted ways, they will be less likely to act out when it isn't appropriate.

- **Spread Out** – Rather than keeping your boys confined to a desk, let them spread out at a table, on the floor, or on the couch. If you allow your boys to move around a bit while doing their book work or papers, you will find that they will get their work done more quickly and with less resistance.

- **Silly Stuff** – If you're finding it hard to hold the attention of your sons, try speaking in a silly voice or acting goofy as you are presenting the information. Injecting a little bit of unexpected humor into your presentations can grab and hold the interest of boys.

- **Talk Breaks** – Provide frequent talk breaks for your boys to minimize disruptions while you're trying to teach. Boys have lots of questions – make sure you give them opportunities to ask these questions and to probe as deeply into a topic as they would like.

- **Visuals** – Use lots of visuals to maintain interest. Most boys learn visually, so seeing the information will make it easier for them to learn than just hearing the information.

Incorporate these tips into your school day and watch the attention span of boys in your house increase. With a little bit of creativity, homeschooling boys can be a rewarding experience for both you and your sons.

Nurturing Competent Communicators

How do most children learn to communicate? The number one way that most modern kids learn language patterns is from media: TV, video games, computers, telephones, texting, etc. Unfortunately, kids are not hearing excellent speech patterns from these sources.

A better way for them to learn language patterns is by having conversations with their parents and other adults. Unfortunately, most of us don't take the time to have deep, meaningful conversations with our children on a regular basis. Technology pulls our family members to opposite corners of our houses and puts ear buds in our ears. We need to be intentional about nurturing competent communicators.

Fortunately, homeschool kids are often voracious readers. Good books can be an excellent source of reliably correct and sophisticated language patterns. The problem with this method is that most good readers read so rapidly that they actually skim through the books. When people read that quickly, the brain is not always able to store the complete language patterns that they encounter.

So what's the solution? We'd all love to raise children with excellent communication skills – children who are able to speak their mind as well as to write down their thoughts in a cohesive and impactful way.

> *Technology pulls our family members to opposite corners of our houses and puts ear buds in our ears.*

Andrew Pudewa, founder of The Institute for Excellence in Writing[17], suggests that reading out loud to our children, no matter what their age or reading ability, is the answer to this problem.

Most parents read to their children when they are young. As they grow and are able to read for themselves, however, parents often stop reading to them and merely listen to their children read instead.

This is a mistake, according to Andrew. He says that we should continue reading books which are just above the level at which our children are reading on their own. This will expand their vocabulary as well as the language patterns which are stored in their brains. Both of these components are necessary for our children to become competent communicators.

Andrew suggests reading aloud to your children 2-3 hours a day. In fact, he says that reading out loud to them is so important that if you took a one year sabbatical from any other teaching and simply read to your child 4-5 hours a day, your child would learn

---

[17] http://iew.com/

more and be farther ahead than they would be if you didn't read out loud to them at all and taught them all of the other subjects as usual.

Sally Clarkson, the author of **Educating the Wholehearted Child**[18] agrees with Andrew on the importance of continuing to read aloud to your children. She recommends that you start your homeschool day by reading aloud to your children and fit in the other subjects as there is time.

I love to read and I love to read aloud to my boys. I used to struggle with having enough time to fit reading aloud into our school day. The other subjects always seemed to expand to fill whatever amount of time we wanted to spend on schoolwork – and there was rarely time to fit reading aloud into our schedule.

After hearing Andrew and Sally's viewpoint on the importance of reading aloud, I switched our days around and started reading aloud to my boys first. This has worked well for us and I have been doing it this way for the past couple of years. My boys and I love it! I let my boys wake up to the gentle subject of hearing books read aloud. Starting our days this way helps us to immediately connect with each other on a deeper level.

Andrew suggests reading books that were written between the years 1840-1920. This is considered to be the golden age of modern English literature. He says that books from this time period have the most linguistic value for your children.

---

[18] Educating the Wholehearted Child by Sally Clarkson

You can also harness the power of media by letting your children listen to audio books. This is also a great activity we've discovered for making long car drives feel much shorter. Audio books are a valuable resource.

Two great resources that I use for choosing great read aloud books are ***Honey for a Child's Heart***[19] by Gladys Hunt and ***Read for the Heart***[20] by Sarah Clarkson.

Try reading aloud to your children at the beginning of your homeschool day, no matter what their age or reading ability. I think you'll find, as I have, that it is time well spent.

---

[19] Honey for a Child's Heart by Gladys Hunt
[20] Read for the Heart by Sarah Clarkson

Yes, Homeschoolers DO Experience Peer Pressure!

When my oldest son was 14, he and I got into quite a lengthy and somewhat heated discussion on the way to church one night. It started right before we jumped into the van. I saw that he didn't have his Bible in his hands, so I said, "Hey, don't forget to bring your Bible." He acted like he heard me; but, then proceeded out the door and got into the van empty handed.

I followed him to the van and said, "Hey, you need your Bible." He was unhappy about it but he did go back and grab it.

The 20 minute ride to church was then filled with the strange and upsetting conversation of me trying to convince my son that he needs to bring his Bible to church. My husband had to work late that night so it was just the boys and me in the van.

My son said that they had Bibles in the classrooms that everyone used so it wasn't necessary for him to bring his… that everyone just used those. He said that the leaders didn't tell them they

HAD to bring their Bibles so they didn't care whether he did or not. He said lots of things that didn't make any sense to me.

Finally, as we were approaching church, he confessed in a weak voice, "Mom, if you make me bring my Bible to church I'll be the only guy my age that does it. I already feel like I don't fit in..."

Ouch! There it was... He was protesting because he wanted to fit in with the other guys his age. And apparently, the other guys his age in youth group don't bring their Bibles to church anymore.

You might think that your son is safe from peer pressure because you homeschool; but, chances are, he probably attends some activity or other where he is experiencing the pressure to "fit in." We all want to feel like we are part of the group. We all want to be liked. We all want to have friends and feel that we have somewhere we belong.

> *" I already feel like I don't fit in..."*

Even us homeschool moms have probably felt that pressure along the way. We compare ourselves to other homeschool moms all the time – even when we're trying not to. We feel pressured to be using the right curriculum, to do enough extracurricular activities, to make food and cleaning products from scratch... or whatever else other homeschool moms around us are doing. And you've probably felt that nagging feeling at church or other places that you don't quite fit in with everyone else because you've bucked the system and are homeschooling your children.

Pressure to conform is hard to resist!

Fortunately, as homeschoolers we do have a lot more control over who our kids spend time with… so we can minimize the negative peer pressure to which they are exposed. Unless we're going to keep them at home for the rest of their lives, however, our kids will experience peer pressure.

Here are 5 Ways to Help Our Kids Handle Peer Pressure:

1. Stand firm – We need to teach our kids to do what God would want them to do rather than what man would want them to do. This is a hard one because no one wants to stand out negatively in their peers' eyes. Practice various situations they might encounter so that they have some idea of how to respond when they are in these situations.

2. Be the bad guy – Give your child permission to blame you for his behavior. Sometimes it's easier to say that he can't do something because his parents won't let him versus the fact that he personally doesn't want to do something. Be his "out."

3. Give them permission – If your child finds himself in a situation he doesn't feel like he can handle, tell him to call you and you will pick him up no questions asked. Some families have code words so that kids can let their parents know what's going on without having to say something embarrassing in front of their friends – or without having to lie.

4. Get out of there! – If bullying is taking place, you might want to evaluate whether or not your family should continue participating in the group. The emotional damage which takes place when being bullied can be hard to overcome. No activity is worth your child becoming depressed or despondent.

5. Advise them – don't always give orders – At some point, we need to let our kids know what we think they should do and then back up and give them room to make their own mistakes. If we never allow our kids to decide anything while they live with us, they will be more likely to make some life-alteringly bad mistakes once they're on their own.
Mistakes are how our kids learn! (My husband has to remind me of this one all the time.)

In my son's case, I did end up letting him keep his Bible in the van and walk into church empty handed. Going to church without his Bible wasn't a sin issue – and I didn't want him to have another reason to feel like he didn't fit in.

> *Mistakes are how our kids learn!*

That night, when I was tucking my son into bed, he said he was sorry that he had talked to me the way he had. He also said he would start bringing his Bible to church.

He did ask if he could get a new, smaller Bible that looked more grown up than the one he had been carrying for years. We were happy to take him to the Christian bookstore to get him a new Bible.

Just recently, when this same son went on a camping trip with his grandpa and all of the grandsons, I noticed that he grabbed his Bible and stuck it in his bag without me telling him to... and without him even letting me know. Praise the Lord, he's growing up!

Peer pressure is tough! Simply by homeschooling them, we are making our kids feel like they don't fit in with quite a few groups in life. Unfortunately, this is even true at many of our churches. Homeschooling our kids is a good thing – but it doesn't always feel that way to them when they're around their publicly schooled friends.

Be sure you spend lots of time talking with your son to find out what struggles he is having and what pressures he is facing. Standing up to peer pressure is hard – even as an adult.

We need to do everything we can to give our kids the tools they need to learn how to stand firm under pressure and do what's right no matter what! But we also need to remember that it's a process. Our sons aren't necessarily going to stand up well under peer pressure until they've developed the self confidence they need to do so. Being a teen is hard!

The 5 Most Important Things to Teach Your Child

They Don't Come From Books

When my stepmom finally lost her long battle with ovarian cancer and went to be with the Lord, our family went through several busy and emotional weeks. We had lot of activities added to the calendar that we weren't expecting... such as helping my dad clean out her personal items, planning the service, the visitation, and the funeral.

As you can imagine, those weeks did not go according to my prior plans.

During that time, we were supposed to have our last full week of homeschooling before summer break – and because of the circumstances, we didn't crack one book open.

We did, however, learn a lot. We learned about what's really important in life.

More than any books read, math facts learned, or scientific theories understood, these 5 things are the most important things to teach your child:

1. Relationship with God – If this isn't in place, nothing else matters. No matter how academically or athletically or musically accomplished they become, if they don't have a personal relationship with Jesus then it is all for nothing. Help your kids to build a strong relationship with God and everything else in their lives will fall into place.

2. Relationship with Spouse – Your kids need to see you and your spouse communicating well, working together, and loving each other so that they will know how to treat their spouses someday. As they witness the tender moments of you two ministering to each other, they will also benefit greatly from the stability of your relationship.

3. Relationship with Children – It's easy to damage our relationships with our kids by being focused on our role as teacher (or taskmaster.) It's more important that we build strong bonds with our kids than that we insist they complete their math workbooks each year. We need to listen to them… study them, and respect them. Appreciate them for who they are rather than who you wish they were. Help them to become all that God wants them to be.

4. Relationship with Parents – Our kids are watching how we treat our parents. Do we honor them? Do we make time for them? Chances are, the way we treat our parents is the way our kids will someday treat us.

5. Relationship with Others – God wants us to love each other the way we love ourselves. It's important that we teach The Golden Rule to our kids. Make volunteering a family priority. Teach your kids to be bold in their faith. Train them to vote and to be informed about our world. Show them how to be kind to others.

> *We didn't crack one book open. We did, however, learn a lot.*

If we teach our kids these five things, we can be ensured that they will have true success in life. Our relationships are the only things we get to bring with us into eternity. The next time you're tempted to sacrifice one of the above things for something less important, remember what truly matters.

Getting Your Teenager to Wake Up in the Morning

7 Quick Tips

When my boys were little, I couldn't figure out any way to keep them in bed after 5:30 or 6:00 in the morning. As they approached their teen years, however, they began sleeping in later and later in the morning. It became hard to get them out of bed before 7 or 7:30. And finally, over one summer, they began sleeping until 10 am, if I let them.

What's going on?!?

To my surprise, this is completely natural. As young people approach and enter puberty, their circadian rhythms, or "body clocks" shift. This means that most teenagers are unable to fall asleep before 11 pm, even if they are lying in bed for hours.

Should we even be waking up our teenagers?

Combine this information with the fact that most teenagers need a minimum of 8 1/2 to 9 1/2 hours of sleep each night. If our kids are lying in bed for hours before they're able to fall asleep, and then we wake them up at 6 or 7 in the morning, they may not be getting enough sleep to feel rested – or to function well throughout the day.

There are many negative effects associated with our teens not getting enough sleep, such as:

- Less alert
- Unable to think clearly
- Less able to remember or understand what they are being taught
- Poor grades
- Depression
- Exhibit more ADHD symptoms
- Obesity
- Suicidal thoughts

Sleep deprivation can have serious side effects. In fact, you're probably aware that it has been used as a method of torture for many years!

Our teenagers' bodies and minds are changing rapidly. They need their sleep. Because of this, we should consider pushing back the time that we start schoolwork in the morning. Allow your teens to start their day later than their younger brothers and sisters.

Once you do start, you might want to begin with a gentle activity such as listening to a read aloud book while eating breakfast. This will allow your teen's mind to become more alert without being jolted awake in the morning.

Either that, or allow your child to do something physically active to get their mind up and running. My boys often enjoy doing Phys Ed before they do anything else!

And what about those times when we need out teens to get out of bed earlier in the morning… or when we are struggling to get them to wake up any time before noon, which just isn't practical on a daily basis.

Here are 7 Quick Tips for Getting Your Teenager to Wake Up in the Morning:

1. Be careful about caffeine – Many teens rely on caffeine and/or sugar to wake up and give them energy when they feel themselves dragging. The problem with using these substances to "wake up" is that the effects are fleeting and can leave the person feeling even worse after they wear off. Also, consuming caffeine after noon can interfere with a person's sleep patterns, making their daytime sleepiness even worse.

2. Vigorous Exercise – Be sure your child gets some vigorous physical exercise during the day. The more physically tired he is when it's time for bed, the easier it will be for him to fall asleep without as much delay.

3. Supplements – There are some natural supplements which can help a person to fall asleep more easily. Melatonin, magnesium, chamomile tea… even a glass of warm milk can help your child to feel more drowsy and ready to go to sleep at night.

4. Regular Bedtimes – Try to have your teen go to bed and wake up at the same time every day – including weekends. This regular schedule helps our bodies to be more prepared for falling asleep at the desired time than if bedtimes change drastically from night to night.

5. Wind Down at Night – Be sure to give your teen time to wind down at night. A warm shower or bath with Epsom salts works wonders. Also, consider having your child read a relaxing book before bed versus watching an exciting show on TV or playing an action packed video game.

6. Adjust the lighting – Try dimming the lights at night or closing the shades. Also, turn on bright lights in the morning. These simple cues will help your child's body to get the signal that it's time to go to sleep or time to wake up.

7. Give him something to look forward to – I'm sure you've noticed that if your child is going to do something exciting that day, he wakes up fairly willingly. If your teen knows that he needs to start his schoolwork immediately upon waking up, you'll have a harder time prying him out of bed than if he knows he has half an hour of free time before he needs to get started.
 Try to give him something exciting that will happen after he gets up – even if that just means making him his favorite breakfast or letting him play a few minutes of his favorite app.

Getting teenagers to wake up in the morning can be difficult. But remember, this too shall pass. Once your teen makes it through this stage of life, they will naturally begin to wake up earlier again.

Hopefully, knowing why they are having such a hard time waking up, and realizing that it's normal, will make things a little bit easier for you in the mornings.

Our Grand Experiment

When my boys were 13 and 14, I started homeschooling them quite a bit differently. I called it Our Grand Experiment! These changes were so radical to me that when I attempted them, I felt that either it was a genius idea – or it would be our downfall.

After reading about tweens and teens and how their sleep cycles change during that phase of life, I decided we needed to do something differently around our house. I had discovered that when I wake my boys up before they're ready to be woken up, they're surly. They both complained that they didn't sleep well, and it took a long time for them to be able to function properly. And when my boys were grumpy then I got grumpy.

So, that year, I tried something radically different!

First, I stopped waking my boys up in the morning.

Yes, you read that right. I decided to try letting them wake up on their own and start their schoolwork whenever they were ready.

This was a challenge for me because I'm the type of person who would rather get up at a decent hour and dive right into our day.

I'd much rather get the vast majority of our work done in the morning so that we are free to do whatever we'd like to do with our afternoons.

When my boys were younger, this system worked well for us. But once they were older, they stumbled through their mornings bleary-eyed... and afternoons appeared to be a better time for them to do their schoolwork.

Next, I started giving my boys a list of schoolwork for the week and let them manage their own time.

This was also a hard one for me. I'm used to giving my boys a list of things I want done for each day... but then, I found myself having to push them from one activity to the next because it felt like they were dawdling and wasting all of our time.

I asked both of my sons if they'd like me to give them a list of everything they needed to get done for the week and they can do as much or as little as they'd like to do each day. They both eagerly agreed that they'd like to make that change.

I was excited and told them that if they worked really hard the first few days of each week, then they could have a day or two to focus on whatever they wanted to learn about. They'd have lots of time to explore whatever their hearts desired.

My boys responded to me with, "If we get all of our work done early can we have lots of time to do NOTHING!?!" I thought about it for a minute and then I told them that if "doing nothing" is what motivated them to get their work done, I guess that would be fine.

There were some rules they needed to follow.

I told my boys that they needed to have all of their schoolwork done by the time Dad gots home from work on Friday... or I would jump back in and help them manage their time more wisely. Also, if that happened, they would be expected to finish whatever they didn't complete during the week on Saturday. UGH!

So, how did it go?

After following this new way of doing things for a couple of weeks, I was happy with Our Grand Experiment! One of my boys woke up at 8am the first day and started immediately working his way through his list. The first thing he did was to spend two hours doing Phys Ed. Seriously. Then, he did some science, and some reading.

> *"If we get all of our work done early can we have lots of time to do NOTHING!?!"*

My other son slept in until around 10:30. He didn't get very much done his first day, which was worrisome to me. After that, however, he kicked things into gear and started working hard to be sure he'd get all of his stuff done before the end of the day on Friday.

At the end of the first week, one of my sons had completed everything by 11am on Friday – and the other one had to scramble to get everything done later into Friday afternoon. But overall, it was a great success. I did talk with one son about how he hadn't used his time well at the beginning of the week. Amazingly, he agreed and talked to me about how he would do things differently the next week.

What did I learn from this experiment?

- My boys' favorite subject is Phys Ed!

- My boys would rather focus on one subject for a longer period of time than to spend short bits of time each day on different subjects. For example, my sons sat down and read 10 chapters of the book they were reading for literature in one sitting versus reading 2 chapters a day, like I would normally assign. Or they'd do all of their math lessons for the week in one sitting rather than doing a lesson each day.

- My boys may dawdle at the beginning of the week – but they do get their work done… and they speed up as their deadline approaches!

- If I trust them and let them move forward at their own pace, it is much more relaxing for them AND for me.

This new way of doing things was a radical change for me. It was counter-intuitive for sure! But it went well for us. My boys learned to manage their own time, they got their work done, they were getting plenty of sleep, and everyone was in a better mood.

I learned to take advantage of my alone time in the mornings rather than in the afternoons. And I learned to back off while my boys picked up more and more responsibility for their own learning.

Making this change did have a few hitches… There were a few Saturdays when one son would have to finish up his work… which he didn't like one little bit. But other than that, this new system worked incredibly well.

We followed this system for an entire year and we were all happy with how things turned out. Our plan is to use this same system for the coming year as well.

If you've always homeschooled a certain way, try talking to your kids to see if they have any suggestions which might make things go more smoothly at your house. Because our kids aren't always wired the same way that we are – you might be amazed at some of the changes you could make that will revolutionize their homeschool experience for the better.

"You Were Right, Mom!"

5 Things Kids Learn from Natural Consequences

I dream of the day when I will hear the words, "You were right, Mom!" escape from either one of my son's lips. That day may not come for a long, long time… but I have been seeing several areas where their actions are telling me that they're starting to agree with me in certain areas.

When my boys were 13 and 14, I began running our homeschool differently. (I describe these differences in the previous chapter called "Our Grand Experiment.") After a few months of not waking up my boys and letting them manage their own time while homeschooling, I saw a lot of growth in my boys.

I think that one of the huge reasons we saw a change in our boys' attitudes and behavior is because of the power of natural consequences.

I first remember hearing about natural consequences while reading Dr. Kevin Leman's book, **Have a New Kid by Friday**[21]. In this book, Kevin talks about how kids learn best when they are allowed to experience the sting of the natural consequences from their behavior.

Some examples of natural consequences would be things like this:

- A child refuses to get dressed for church so he goes to church with his pajamas on.
- A child refuses to eat the food which is served so he goes hungry.

- A teen refuses to wear a coat when going on a youth group trip so he will get cold.

- An adult is chronically late for work and he doesn't receive a hoped for promotion.

As you can see, both adults and kids can learn from the consequences of their behavior. Learning from natural consequences is much more effective than learning from a mom nagging or yelling at you when you don't do what you're supposed to do. I was happy with the changes I saw in my boys as a result of natural consequences.

---

[21] Have a New Kid by Friday by Dr. Kevin Leman

Here are 5 Things My Boys Learned from Natural Consequences:

1. Wake me up – Instead of wanting to sleep the day away, one of my sons specifically asked me to start waking him up in the morning. He wanted to get up at 8 am so that he had plenty of time to get his schoolwork done before lunchtime. Turns out, he missed having his free time in the afternoon and he decided that "10 am really is too late to sleep in."

Not only that, but when we went through the time change that fall, he wanted me to start waking him up at 7 am instead. I'm telling you, this is nothing short of a miracle!

2. Spread out the hard subjects – When we first started letting the boys choose when they worked on each subject, they tended to save up all of their math, Latin, and writing for Friday. That made Fridays very painful! It also made it much more likely that they would have to finish up their work either Friday night or Saturday.

> *He missed having his free time in the afternoon and he decided that "10 am really is too late to sleep in."*

After having that happen a few times, my boys both started trying to spread out their hard subjects a bit more. They decided that one math lesson per day tends to work best. Latin words are much easier to learn when you actually practice them every day. And you can come up with quality papers when you give yourself time to think through your assignments before attempting to get your words on paper.

3. Checklists are helpful – My sons used to balk at the fact that I wanted them to check off each subject after they had completed it for the day. Once they had one checklist for the entire week, however, they quickly realized just how helpful checklists can actually be.

After just a few weeks, one of my sons told me how good it feels to be able to look back at his weekly checklist and see all of the things that he had completed that week. He said it felt satisfying. Yep. I feel the same way, son!

4. Easing into the week is kinda nice – We've gotten into a rhythm where my boys have been enjoying spending the majority of their time on Mondays and Tuesdays doing their reading for the week. They are usually tired on Mondays because weekends are often busy in our household. I think I'm the one who is learning this lesson. I'm learning that Mondays can be less painful and my boys will still get their schoolwork done by the end of the week.

5. Saturdays stink when you haven't finished your schoolwork – Fortunately, it didn't take many Saturdays of having left over schoolwork for my boys to figure this one out. Who wants to do math on a Saturday?!? No one at my house does, anyway. My boys have learned that it's much less painful to get your schoolwork done during the week than to lollygag around and have to complete it on the weekend.

These lessons are being learned naturally without me having to incessantly nag or lecture them. I can't tell you how nice that has been for all of us. Instead of feeling like I need to follow behind them and hurry them along, I've been sitting back and letting them choose how hard they will work each day. When they choose wisely, they reap the benefits. When they choose poorly, they suffer the consequences.

6 Important Considerations for Raising Engaged Citizens

If you live in a country where you have the privilege of voting, it's so important that you take advantage of this opportunity. Homeschooling used to be illegal in many countries, including America. We are always one election away from losing all of the hard fought for educational freedoms that we hold dear.

Each year on Election Day I think about how important it is that we raise our kids to be engaged citizens. As many of their peers are being indoctrinated in school, it becomes even more important for our children to be able to stand against the tide, to vote for people who hold the same Christian principles as we do, and to stand up for what's right in a society which is increasingly embracing whatever feels good.

Here are 6 Important Considerations for Raising Engaged Citizens:

1. **Firm Foundation** – We must raise our children to not only believe in God, but to have a deep knowledge of who He is.

Immerse them in the Bible. Help them to become familiar with catechism for whichever denomination you see fit. Be sure to study apologetics with them so that they also understand WHY they believe what they believe. Help them to be able to think through their faith so that it becomes something they own and not just something their parents believe.

> *We are always one election away from losing all of the hard fought for educational freedoms that we hold dear.*

If your kids are middle school or high school age, you may want to go through the Summit Ministries[22] worldview curriculum with your kids. We have found their materials to be thorough and engaging!

2. Be Aware – It's important that our kids know and understand what's going on in the world around them. Watch the news with them. Discuss current events. Point out what's going on in your community. Compare what they're seeing in the world around us with what God lays out in His Word. A good tool we've recently discovered is **CNN Student News**[23]. This is a non partisan news program for students which does a great job of being entertaining as well as informative.

3. Be Informed – It's also important that our kids have a good grasp of history. We need to be careful when teaching our kids history. So many textbooks are presenting revisionist history to our kids.

---

[22] http://www.summit.org/curriculum/
[23] http://www.cnn.com/studentnews

For accurate historical materials, I recommend Wallbuilders[24], The Providence Foundation[25], and ***The Light and the Glory***[26] series (adult version or young readers version.) Also, you may want to consider sticking to books rather than textbooks while teaching this important subject. Do your research before presenting the materials to your kids to be sure they are learning accurate history. If you prefer using textbooks, check out Notgrass History.[27]

4. Reach Out – Engaged citizens care about the world around them. Volunteer with your kids. Teach them to pray for others. Help them to develop a caring spirit for the people around them.

5. Speak Out – Our kids need to know that it's important for them to stand up for what's right. Help them to be comfortable speaking their mind respectfully. Teach them to ask good questions. Speech classes are a great experience whenever possible. It's not enough for our kids to know what's right – they need to be willing to share that information with others. This also includes sharing the gospel message!

6. Vote – In America, as well as many other countries, we have the precious privilege of being able to have a voice in our government. We need to exercise that right whenever it's available. Take your kids to vote with you. Make it a big deal, no matter how small the election. Watch the returns coming in on TV with them. View and discuss presidential debates with

---

[24] www.wallbuilders.com (David Barton)
[25] www.providencefoundation.com
[26] The Light and the Glory series by Peter Marshall and David Manuel
[27] http://www.notgrass.com/notgrass/

them. Study government so that your kids understand how it all works and how vital it is that they participate.

It's important that we prepare our kids to be engaged citizens someday. We must always remember the huge sacrifices made by so many to give us the right to vote. Please teach your kids to advantage of this important opportunity!

Better Late Than Early?

When Should We Start Teaching Our Children?

Is it better if we start educating our kids when they are as young as 2 or 3? Or is it better if we wait until they are as old as 8 or 9? You've probably heard both sides of the argument. Many childhood experts have begun encouraging us parents to send our 3-year-olds off to preschool.

Start them early

"I believe that all three- or four-year-olds should have the opportunity and advantages of attending preschool," says Anna Jane Hays, a child development expert in Santa Fe and author of several books, including **Ready, Set, Preschool!**[28] and **Kindergarten Countdown**[29]. "It's just too valuable of a beginning, now that we know children are capable of learning at such an early age. The consensus is 'the sooner, the better' in regard to a structured opportunity for learning."

---

[28] Ready, Set, Preschool by Anna Jane Hays
[29] Kindergarten Countdown by Anna Jane Hays

Wait to start them

On the other hand, Dr. Raymond Moore, one of the first homeschooling pioneers and author of ***Better Late than Early***[30] would advocate waiting until your child is between the ages of 8-12 before sending him off to school. His stance was that boys in particular aren't ready to read as early as our schools would like them to be. He suggested waiting until our children are older to start a formal education with them. This gives them time for their maturity and logical skills to be ready to tackle their schoolwork.

(By the way, Raymond Moore does recommend working with your children at a young age if they appear to be ready. He just doesn't recommend sending them off to school until they are older than the age he recommends.)

So, with experts lining up on both sides of the issue, what should homeschooling parents do? Should we start teaching our children when they are young or should we wait until they're older to start working with them on their lessons?

No matter which expert you agree with, you can't stop your child from learning.

Babies are learning before they are even born! Young children are always learning. They learn how to sit up, to crawl, and to walk. They learn how to understand language and how to talk. They are learning how to control their bodies. Learning is

---

[30] Better Late Than Early by Dr. Raymond Moore

always going on in the lives of our children – whether they know it or not.

I started teaching my boys "school" lessons when my oldest son was almost 2 years old. This does not mean that I sat them down with a stack of worksheets and made them sit still and write for hours at a time. In fact, they probably didn't realize that anything had changed in our house.

Things had changed for me, however. Instead of randomly playing with my sons and trying to find stuff to do to keep us busy, I now had a plan. I started coming up with fun lessons for us to focus on throughout the week – sort of like unit studies for toddlers or preschoolers.

One week we would learn about astronauts and space. The next week we would learn about bugs and spiders. We read stacks and stacks of books. We worked on fine motor skills and gross motor skills. We covered the ABCs and 123s. They ran and jumped and tried new foods and used all of their senses to explore the world around them.

The subject of the lessons weren't really the point. The point was that we were having fun together. I had a plan to follow. And my sons were discovering that learning was fun.

No matter what age you are, sitting down for too long is bad for your health. We shouldn't expect our kids to sit still for hours at a time while we try to teach them. In fact, moving and learning go hand in hand. Our kids need to move almost as much as they need to breathe. We should be building physical activity into their day no matter what their age.

Through teaching these lessons to my boys, I came up with ***Learn & Grow: Hands-On Lessons for Active Preschoolers***[31]. In these lessons, kids learn by jumping around, reading books, laughing, and throwing stuff. They aren't forced to sit still for long periods of time.

Kids learn better when they're moving, anyway – especially boys.

Our kids need to move almost as much as they need to breathe.

Better late than early? Depends on what kind of learning you're talking about. If you're planning to use textbooks and stacks of worksheets then you should wait until they're older to start educating your kids. If you're planning to use fun, hands-on learning then in my opinion you cannot start too soon.

Don't make your kids sit at a desk with a pencil in their hand all day.

When kids are experiencing our world first hand you can't stop them from learning. You can, however, direct their learning and join them in it. As you teach your children, no matter what age you start, you will get to experience the joy of watching them "get it" for the first time... day after day.

---

[31] http://www.homeschool-your-boys.com/learnandgrowpreschoolcurriculum.html

Four Questions to Avoid a One Size Fits All Education

One type of education does not fit all. Our kids are unique. They all have different learning styles, different interests, different strengths and different weaknesses. So why do we think that we can give them all the same education and have it work? Why would we even want to do this?

Here are some reasons we might be tempted to try giving our kids a one size fits all education:

- That's the kind of education we received and it feels comfortable

- We want to do "school at home" to be sure our kids are able to get into college

- We've already purchased a curriculum and it worked for our older kids

- We don't know any better

- We aren't sure how we could teach all of our kids different things with a finite number of hours in each day

As you can see, there are some valid reasons for why parents begin educating kids in this manner. It's easy to fall into this trap.

You begin using a curriculum with your kids and you think everything is going along fine… until suddenly the kids start making faces and seem like they'd rather do just about anything than to have to do their schoolwork. Have you ever heard your sons say, "This is stupid! I'll never use this?!?!"

This has happened at our house. My goal has always been to help my boys love learning. I've spent a lot of time trying to craft their lessons so that they would be inspirational as well as educational. As they've gotten older, however, this has become more difficult.

Neither of my boys enjoys math at all. In fact, they actually hate it. They think it's a complete waste of time. One of my sons is pretty good at math and is actually ahead of where he would be if he were in public school. The other son is probably behind where he would be.

The farther this son "falls behind," the more pressure I felt to try to get him "caught up." After all, everywhere you look there are experts telling us how important it is for our kids to excel in the STEM classes (Science, Technology, Engineering, and Math.) And math isn't a subject you can get away with skipping completely, no matter how badly you or your child might want to.

So, my husband and I devised a scheme to try to get our son farther ahead in math. We started having him do math every day all year round. Yes, doing math seems to be torture for this boy – but we were trying to help him get better at it so we felt we needed to really push him in this area. Every day school became hard because as soon as this son had to do math, he was upset.

Then, I heard a podcast by Michael Hyatt, a leadership and productivity expert. The podcast was called ***Operating in your Strengths Zone***[32]. In the podcast, he tells the story of Daniel "Rudy" Ruettiger, which was portrayed in the movie ***Rudy***[33] back in 1993. You may have seen the movie; but, just in case you haven't, it basically tells the story of a guy named Rudy who desperately wants to play football for Notre Dame.

Long story short, Rudy works hard to try to overcome his low grades and his lack of natural football talent. At the end of the movie, Rudy is able to go on the field for one play and he is thrilled. I watched that movie myself when it came out and viewed it as a super inspirational movie.

Michael Hyatt's take on it, however, was that Rudy had put a tremendous amount of effort into trying to overcome his shortcomings and that he was only able to have limited success. He said that if he had worked that hard improving his strengths, it would have made a much greater difference in his life and in the lives of others.

---

[32] www.michaelhyatt.com – podcast episode #023
[33] Rudy (movie)

Michael quoted Marcus Buckingham and Donald Clifton's bestseller, ***Now, Discover Your Strengths***[34], with this amazing statement:

> *"No matter how hard you try, you really can't improve your weaknesses. You are wasting time and energy trying to do so. The best thing you can do is discover your strengths and then find a role that allows you to use them."*

Wow! When I heard that, it blew me away. Why were we focusing so hard on my son's weakness in math when we should instead be focusing on his strengths?!? Like I said before, we can't just ditch math. But we didn't have to put such an inordinate emphasis on it.

> ***If he had worked that hard improving his strengths, it would have made a much greater difference in his life and in the lives of others.***

Since that time, we have switched things up. Our sons are doing math 3 days a week rather than every day. We are learning logic with them on the off days, which is something they both enjoy! They have also been able to spend more time learning speech skills, computer skills, filmmaking skills, and entrepreneurial skills with the time we've freed up.

When we focus on teaching our sons things that they enjoy, they aren't going to feel like they're wasting their time learning things they will never use.

---

[34] Now, Discover Your Strengths by Marcus Buckingham and Donald Clifton

We need to spend the majority of our time teaching our kids with the following in mind:

- What are their interests?

- What are their learning styles?

- What are their strengths?

- How do you need to prepare them for careers you could actually see them doing?

Tricia Goyer wrote a wonderful post called *Why Your Older Kids Fight Your Teaching… and How to Fix That*[35].

She lists three questions that I think are vital for us to ask if we're going to provide our kids with the best type of education for them:

1. If there were no "standards" for your child to follow what would he or she enjoy learning?

2. What would be an effective way to get your child more excited about learning?

3. What could you do to draw your child's heart toward God?

I love those questions. I especially love this one: **What would you teach if there were no standards?**

---

[35] www.triciagoyer.com

We need to think about these questions when we are developing a plan for our homeschools so that we will be preparing our sons for what God has in store for their lives – rather than trying to give them a Plain Jane, one size fits all education which could destroy their love for learning.

My son will never be a mathematician or anything which forces him to use large amounts of math every day. But he will have more time to discover what he's good at now that we aren't forcing him to focus on a subject which confounds him quite so much.

We need to try to ignite our kids' passions rather than dull their senses by trying to pack their brains full of meaningless facts and figures. Give your son an education which is tailor made for him and you won't hear him complaining as much that he'll never use what he's learning.

Give Yourself a Break!

8 Ways to Regain Enthusiastic Learning

I'm not the kind of person who thinks about taking breaks often enough. When things get difficult, I'd much rather keep on pushing through the pain than take some time off to rest. I see the finish line and I don't want to stop until I bust through the tape. The more tired I feel, the more of an urge I have to double down and increase my speed.

I do not recommend this approach, by the way. It's a great way to cause myself and my boys to get burned out.

By March each year, many of us homeschool moms hit that time of year when we're less than enthusiastic about teaching lessons. For those of us in northern climates, the cold, gloomy winter weather can feel quite oppressive. The kids spend less time outside so they have a hard time burning off their extra energy making our homes exponentially louder. We see sunshine infrequently causing us to feel tired. The air in our closed-up houses is beginning to smell stale. Can you tell how badly I'm yearning for spring as I'm writing this!?!

Even if you're over halfway done with the school year at that point, you may find that even that thought doesn't make you feel more energized. When you find yourself in the doldrums of the year, you would be wise to give yourself a break.

If you don't give yourself a break every once in awhile, you may find that God will impose one on you. We had that happen to us one year.

First, we found out that my step-mom's ovarian cancer had spread throughout her body and that she only had a few months to live. In the light of that news, completing a certain amount of schoolwork each week didn't seem anywhere near as important as being there for family.

> *If you don't give yourself a break every once in awhile, you may find that God will impose one on you.*

A few days after receiving that news, my boys both came down with the stomach flu. As soon as they got sick, we found ourselves taking a break from ALL schoolwork for the week. It didn't start out as a relaxing break – but it did end up being rejuvenating as we all ended up catching up on our sleep and having a restful week stuck at home.

In retrospect, I wish I had been smart enough to take an intentional break that we could have enjoyed a bit more rather than God having to force one on us!

If you find yourself in need of a break, here are 8 ways to regain everyone's enthusiasm for learning:

1. Put down the regular books and give a unit study a try. This is a great way to shake up your regular routine if things are feeling stale.

2. Let your kids choose something that interests them and help them to do a deep study about that one thing versus being pulled in many directions throughout the day.

3. Declare a reading day. Let the kids read books that THEY choose for themselves.

4. Go on a fun field trip. Be sure to get feedback from your kids on where they'd like to go.

5. Take a day (or a week) off of schoolwork. Let everyone have some time to do whatever they want.

6. Watch a movie. If you're really adventurous, you can even watch something that ISN'T educational!

7. Get together with friends.

8. Play video games together as a family.

Don't be afraid to put down the regular books and try some more adventurous learning – or even give formal learning a vacation for a time.

A college in our area gives their students the month of January off of their regular studies so that they can attend a 3-week lecture series. This break allows the students to become inspired by the speakers as well as to give their brains a break from their rigorous study schedule.

If a college can see the benefit of giving their students time off, certainly us homeschool moms should also be willing to give our younger kiddos occasional breaks now and then.

The next time you or your kids feel drained, try planning a restorative break. Sometimes, just having something to look forward to is enough to help everyone focus on and enjoy their regular studies again.

Develop a Motivation to Learn in Your Sons!

High levels of motivation to learn will automatically develop in your children when they are treated well, respected, encouraged, and when their schoolwork has meaning for them. Homeschool moms and dads who understand how to motivate a student can greatly enhance the education experience and performance of their children.

Most homeschooled boys are bright and inquisitive and have a high motivation to learn – but all children go through phases when they are uninterested or lazy. If you find your child in one of these stages, do not despair. There are many things you can do to try to regain your child's excitement for learning.

Ways to Increase a Student's Motivation to Learn:

- **Achievable Goals** – Encourage your boys to focus on their continued improvement, not just on their grade for any one test or assignment. Help them evaluate their progress by encouraging them to critique their own work, analyze their strengths, and work on their weaknesses.

- **Difficulty Level** – Ensure opportunities for your son's success by assigning tasks that are neither too easy nor too difficult. If the work is boring and he already understands, let him move on to the next assignment.

- **Enthusiasm** – An instructor's enthusiasm is a crucial factor in a student's motivation to learn. If you act bored or apathetic, your children will too. Challenge yourself to think of the most exciting way to present the material to your children.

- **Fast Feedback** – Give your boys feedback as quickly as possible. Return tests and papers promptly, and reward success publicly and immediately. Brag to dad or the grandparents about how well your kids have done on an assignment. Give students some indication of how well they have done and how to improve. Rewards can be as simple as saying a child's response was good, with an indication of why it was good. Giving frequent, early, positive feedback will support a student's belief that they can do well. This also saves you from grading papers at night!

- **Fun** – Boys love sports because they are fun, exciting, sometimes thrilling, and highly emotional. Learning experiences for boys can and should provide just as much enjoyment and satisfaction as do sports. We sometimes think that certain learning tasks are boring by necessity (like memorization of definitions, grammar, vocabulary or spelling), but sometimes this might just reflect a lack of creativity on our part. If we put Bible verses or spelling words to song, they can be a lot of fun to learn. Allow your kids to throw a ball back and forth while they practice spelling words. Use your imagination and you can make learning fun for your sons.

- **High Expectations** – Hold high but realistic expectations for your students. Research has shown that a teacher's expectations have a powerful effect on a student's performance. If you act as though you expect your students to be motivated, hardworking, and interested in the material, they are more likely to be so.

- **Increase Difficulty Progressively** – Ensure that the task is of an appropriate level of challenge for your child's age and ability level. If it is too easy the student will be bored and unmotivated. A level of difficulty too high above the student's ability could lead to frustration and him giving up. Give your boys opportunities to succeed at the beginning of the year. Once students feel they can succeed, you can gradually increase the difficulty level. If assignments and exams include easy and hard questions, your child will have a chance to experience success as well as challenge.

- **Outside the Classroom** – It has been said that most learning takes place outside of the classroom. This is good news for homeschoolers! We still need to remember to prime our children to continue learning after they're done with their formal schoolwork, to prepare them to be aware, and to ask them to apply concepts in their lives as they go about their day.

- **Positive Atmosphere** – Create an atmosphere that is open and positive. Praise builds your childrens' self-confidence, competence, and self-esteem. Recognize sincere efforts from your sons even if the product is less than stellar. Use praise liberally.

- **Reward Success** – Reward for effort and improvement and not just for the outcome. When boys play sports, the game provides a constant flow of accomplishments and the enjoyment of those accomplishments. Even the sports team that ultimately loses enjoys an occasional strikeout, a base hit, or a well-caught fly ball. Homeschooling parents should try to replicate this stream of small but constant ego rewards in their son's lessons. Breaking learning into small pieces that can be mastered and that will produce a feeling of accomplishment and success will help motivate students to go forward, even through very difficult material.

- **Strengths and Interests** – The task should be meaningful and relevant to the learner. Students often comment, "Why do I have to learn about _____? I'll never use this when I grow up!?" Find out what your children are interested in and how they feel about the subject matter. Be sure to tailor their lessons so that your boys will also be able to fully explore the subjects that interest them most. Be sure to explain how the content of their schoolwork will help them to achieve their educational, professional, or personal goals.

- **Student Choices** – Students will be more motivated to engage in a task if they have some control over what the task is or how it is to be carried out and presented. The less controlling the teacher, the more motivation to learn the student will have. When possible, let students have some say in choosing what will be studied. Give students options on the subject matter for term papers or other assignments. Let students decide between two locations for a field trip or have them select which topics to explore in greater depth.

- **Teamwork** – People are generally sociable and like being around each other. Kids usually enjoy working as a team; yet, often the learning activities we assign call for individual effort. By working on some team projects with our children, we can take advantage of the benefits of teamwork, where the younger siblings will learn by having the older ones help. And, of course, since teaching someone something is the best way to learn, the students who teach each other will learn better than if they were always learning on their own.

- **Valued** – Help students feel that they are valued members of a learning community. Again, this is natural for homeschoolers as you are teaching your own children, whom you highly value.

- **Vary Activities** – Variety reawakens students' involvement in the material and their motivation. Break up the routine by incorporating a variety of teaching activities and methods throughout the day such as: role playing, brainstorming, discussion, demonstrations, case studies, or small group work.

We should strive to make learning always at least mentally active and often physically active as well. The students should be responsible for producing something, rather than just sitting passively and soaking up the presentation.

Homeschool moms definitely have the ability to increase the motivation to learn in their students. Many of these behaviors come naturally for homeschooling parents; however, if you find your sons lacking motivation, be sure to give some of these suggestions a try!

Fun Elementary Lessons

Use Surprises and Silliness to Motivate Our Kids

A fun way to motivate our kids is to pack our lessons full of surprises and silliness. Positive emotions enhance learning and motivation. Your boys will have strong and lasting memories if they are experiencing intense emotions while they are learning.

If you can make something fun, exciting, happy, loving, or perhaps even a bit frightening, students will learn more readily and the learning will last much longer. You can create emotions while teaching your kids by doing something unexpected or outrageous, by giving praise, and by many other means. **Surprises and silliness make lessons so much more memorable for your boys!**

Fun and unforgettable elementary lessons could be such things as you teaching the class in period costume, acting like a mad scientist when you're doing a science experiment, or having everyone sing their answers. Don't be afraid to embarrass yourself to make a memorable point.

Try motivating your students by using these surprises and silliness techniques:

- **Be Energetic** – Being energetic in your teaching is a motivating factor in itself; adding energy to the ideas you want to convey will further enhance learning and commitment to the ideas.

> *Don't be afraid to embarrass yourself to make a memorable point.*

- **Catch!** – Throw soft candy, like circus peanuts, into your students' mouths if they get the answer right.

- **Crafts** – Let your kids have time to make a fun and unusual craft. This is good for their imagination as well as giving them a break from their traditional book work.

- **Dancing** – Jump up and start dancing during a lesson. Your boys will jump up and join you – it's a great way to get the wiggles out as well as to get the blood pumping when the kids are feeling lethargic.

- **Enthusiasm** – If you become bored or apathetic, students will too. Typically, an instructor's enthusiasm comes from confidence, excitement about the subject, and genuine pleasure in teaching. If you find yourself uninterested in the material, challenge yourself to devise the most exciting way to present the lesson… or teach them about something else!

- **Humor** – Allow your boys to express humor in appropriate ways and at appropriate times. Acknowledge your son's skill at being humorous. Sometimes, you just have to have a sense of humor when the boys are joking around. Don't allow yourself to become annoyed at their antics – be in the right frame of mind and they will brighten up your day.

- **Mud** – Let your sons put on bathing suits and roll around in a bunch of mud if they do their schoolwork well that day. And let them run through the sprinkler to get cleaned up again.

- **Music** – Sing their lessons to them. You can also accompany yourself on a musical instrument that you have at home – whether you know how to play the instrument or not. Have your boys join you in singing the lessons as well.

- **Outside** – Move their desks or table outside without them realizing you've done so and have them do their lessons outdoors for the day. This is a great spring or fall surprise!

- **Pies** – Let students throw a pie in your face if they get 100% on a test.

- **Play Dead** – Have a guest come in and play dead. Let your sons solve the murder mystery. This will help to strengthen their reading and logic skills.

- **Strange Voices** – Use strange voices when you are teaching the lesson. Or, allow your boys to use silly voices when they give their answers.

- **Stunts** – This is a great way for Dad to get involved with homeschooling. Have him offer to have his head shaved or to run a marathon if they achieve a certain level of work.

- **Visual aids** – Use silly pictures or cartoons to get across the point of the lesson.

Different approaches will motivate each child differently. Use your imagination to continue to try new ideas out on your boys, until you discover which methods work best for them.

Fun elementary lessons motivate students and help them to remember the information longer as well. Add surprises and silliness to your lessons and bring the fun back into your boys' learning.

How to Teach Your Son When He Won't Sit Still

I get lots of questions from moms of young boys who have a hard time getting their sons to sit still. Some of these moms don't feel like they are able to teach their sons anything. They are unsure of how to get their sons to slow down long enough to sit through a book, complete a worksheet, or finish their math problems. When your son is extremely active, how do you slow him down long enough to get him to learn?

There are a couple of ways to look at this issue. First, it is natural for boys to want to be on the move. Sitting still for long periods of time isn't a skill that many boys can master, especially when they are young. It is only after spending time working with them that a boys' attention span will slowly increase and they will gain the ability to sit still for any length of time.

As moms, we know that kids need to be taught how to tie their shoes or to complete math problems. For some reason, however, we think they should have been born with the ability to sit still. This is certainly not the case.

The other way to look at this issue is that children don't always need to be sitting still to be learning. In fact, most children learn better when they are moving and doing then when they are sitting and listening. The famous adage, *"I hear and I forget. I see and I remember. I do and I understand"* is certainly true. Most people will learn much more from moving and doing and completing projects than they ever will from sitting and listening or watching someone else do something.

> *Most children learn better when they are moving and doing then when they are sitting and listening.*

Does that mean that if your child can't sit still you don't have to address the issue? Not at all. Sitting still is certainly an important skill to develop. But develop is the operative word. And you need to help your child build up this skill. It may take time – especially for some children for which being still doesn't even come close to coming naturally.

Below are some tips for helping your child acquire the skill of sitting still:

1. **Be patient** – The most important thing to remember is to be patient with your child. Nothing makes a boy more antsy than having his parent angry or frustrated with him. Remember that learning to sit still for any length of time will take time. Take a deep breath when you feel yourself getting frustrated. As you

work on this skill with your son, you will see results. And the more patient you are as you work with your child, the faster all of his skills will develop.

2. Work with him slowly – All skills take time to develop. Sitting still is no exception. Use a timer as a stopwatch to see how long your child can sit still (or glance at the clock if a visible timer makes your child anxious.) Then gradually add a minute at a time until your child is able to sit and listen for longer periods of time. Be sure to reward your child as he makes progress.

3. Give your child something to do – It helps some children tremendously to be able to do something with their hands while listening. Let them build with blocks while they listen, quietly play with letter tiles, rock back and forth on the floor, play cat's cradle or any other mindless activity you can come up with. It might seem like your child isn't paying attention to you if they are doing something else while you read or instruct him; however, often this is not the case. Some kinesthetic learners actually need to be doing something in order to learn or listen properly. Quiz your child and if he is able to answer your questions then his movements are helping and not hindering his learning.

4. **Adapt your curriculum to your child's needs** – If you have a curriculum which is filled with lots of worksheets and your child hates to sit and fill out papers, you may need to make a change. Rather than sounding out letters from a worksheet, make a large letter on the floor with masking tape and let him run on top of it.

Or make a huge object out of cardboard and let your child try to knock it down with a beanbag while he says whatever fact he is supposed to be learning. Or let him jump around the outside of the house or run laps while practicing his spelling words. **Don't be a slave to your curriculum.** Our job is to adapt the curriculum to the needs of our child. This takes some work but it is worth it to see the joy of learning light up our child's face.

5. Purchase a different curriculum – Rather than having to do the work of adapting your current curriculum, you may want to combine a couple or throw out what you have and purchase something new. There are so many options out there that none of us are stuck with one way of teaching our children. Go to homeschool conventions and book fairs until you find something that will work for your child. And remember, just because something worked for one of your children does not mean it will work for the next. Be ready to change for the good of your child!

6. Tips for Reading Books – If it seems painful for your child to listen to you read aloud, try reading picture books with beautiful or interesting illustrations. Read books using lots of expression in your voice. Let your child act out the action of the book as you read. Let him listen to an audio book narrated by a professional voice actor. Choose books which have lots of dramatic or funny events and will interest your child. Again, it is important that you start slowly and work your way up. Rather than thinking your child should be able to start out by sitting through a stack of books, start by reading just one book at a time or even just a few pages if necessary. Let your child take a break and then start back in. Over time, his attention span will increase and you will be amazed by how long he will want to sit and listen to you read.

7. **Make it Fun** – There is no way we can ever teach everything to our children. But we can give them a desire to want to continue learning. If we make learning fun, our children will develop that desire. Talk with eagerness in your voice. Challenge your children with excitement. Give lots of praise. Help them to see and be proud of their accomplishments.

It's important for us to remember that sitting still is not a skill with which many boys are born. Be prepared to work with your children. Over time and with lots of patience, you will start to see their attention span increase and their need for wiggling decrease.

Eventually, your son will learn to sit still. In the meantime, meet your child where he is at and enjoy the journey!

Ignite their Enthusiasm for Learning

Are the lessons you teach your boys inspirational or completely forgettable? I was an attentive student and I earned excellent grades in school. As I think back on my childhood education, however, there are very few lessons that actually stick out in my mind.

I remember the smoking machine that my fifth grade teacher made to show us the dangers of smoking cigarettes. I remember the theoretical wagon train that my eighth grade teacher took us on to teach us about the western migration in America. I remember making rock candy in tenth grade chemistry. I remember dissecting animals (yuck!) in biology.

What do all of these things have in common? They all involved either hands-on activities or essentially acting out the lesson.

> *"The mind is not a vessel to be filled but a fire to be kindled."*
> *– Plutarch*

If this is truly the case, we must find different ways to educate our sons than merely throwing a stack of worksheets in front of them and calling it schoolwork. The minds of our sons are yearning for something more – a way of learning which will satisfy their need for movement as well as ignite a desire to learn in their souls.

There are several ways we can ignite their enthusiasm for learning:

1. Hands-on Activities – Yes, they are messy. Yes, they take time to prepare. Yes, they eat up more time than does filling out a dreaded worksheet. But when he is an adult, will your son be more likely to remember filling in the blanks of History Worksheet Page 86 or launching pumpkins from a life-sized catapult that he built in the backyard?

> *The minds of our sons are yearning for something more...*

Take the time to research and include hands-on activities in your lessons. Boys need to complete real tasks to be able to fully appreciate all of the nuances of a particular subject. Complete the suggested science experiments. Create models. They may take more time – but even a few of these projects each week will make the lessons more real for your sons.

2. Field Trips – If you are studying geography and can visit the place in person, your child will remember it forever. If you are learning about a type of flower that you can find in the woods, it will become more real to your child. If you're studying the industrial age and take a tour of a factory, more information from the lessons will make sense and stick with your child.

It's not always possible to find relevant field trips for everything we study; however, there are lots of parks, museums, historical sites, companies, etc. available to visit. Most of us can take many more field trips than we do. Try fitting a few more field trips into your lesson plans and watch learning come to life.

3. Play Games – Games are always appreciated by boys. If you're teaching them about Native Americans, have them play a game of lacrosse (after they've built their own equipment, of course.) If you're learning about medieval England, let them have a sword fight. If you are reviewing math facts, throw down a bunch of numbers on the floor and let them see who can dive onto the correct answer first. Review any lesson by playing a custom game of Jeopardy. Learning doesn't have to be mundane. Try to keep it lively and fresh!

4. **Videotape or Photos** – Instead of having your son write out what he has just learned, you can occasionally let him tell the information in the form of a news broadcast which you videotape. Or let him create a photo collage of the events.

It's important for kids to be able to communicate by writing down their ideas. It's equally important, however, for them to be able to communicate in other ways such as verbally, visually, etc. Instead of always making them write everything out, try to come up with some creative ways for them to report back what they've learned.

5. Act it Out – If you want to be sure your kids understand their lessons, have them act out what they've learned for you. The more you allow them to get into this by wearing costumes, making sets, etc. the more they will remember. Acting out lessons is a wonderful way to find out what they really learned – and to get those lessons to stick in their heads. And consider videotaping these productions so that the whole family will be able to enjoy the lessons years later.

6. Humor and Silly Voices – When you are reading information to your boys, use silly voices and humorous expressions on occasion. Get your boys to laugh. Who says that every historical figure had a deadpan, slightly bored voice. When reading about an explorer who comes upon a band of Native Americans with arrows trained on them, your voice should register fright. If a character speaks using pompous words, give him a pompous voice. Really go for it! Read with animation. Your boys will appreciate it and be much more apt to remember what they've heard.

7. Mentorships/Internships – Depending on the age of your child, getting him involved with a mentor or an internship of some type is one of the greatest learning experiences of all. This is real world experience! Give him a chance to learn about cars by working on them with a mechanic. Let him learn some biology by observing a veterinarian. These experiences will be life changing and your sons will never be the same. What kinds of skills do their grandparents have? Would they be willing to share some of their life experiences with your kids?

Are the lessons you teach your boys inspirational or completely forgettable? It's never too late to incorporate some additional activities into your lessons and ignite your child's enthusiasm for learning.

Incorporate Games into their Lessons

And Your Younger Boys will Love to Learn

When my sons have been doing their lessons for awhile and I notice that their enthusiasm is gone, I try to think of ways that I can add games to our day. I've found that my sons will do their schoolwork much more rapidly and happily if I'm able to make it seem as if they're playing a game.

Boys like lots of opportunities for physical activity, so these games also make it so they aren't required to sit still for long periods of time.

Try these ideas for making a lesson into a game:

- Have your boys run laps around the house between math problems

- Let them run down the hall, touch the wall, and run back after classifying a sentence.

- Let them compete with a sibling to see who can finish their assignment faster.

- Set a timer and see how long it takes for them to complete a task. Time each math problem and let them compete against their previous time to try to do each math problem more and more quickly.

- Let them somersault off the couch or across the living room floor if they get the answer right.

- Have them play a game of leap frog (while learning about silent letters)

- Let them do a puzzle or a short computer activity between subjects

- Have them jump on a trampoline while answering test questions

- Ask your child to try to come up with a game for learning a specific type of information

- Have your children act out a scene from history. Be sure to use props and costumes if possible. Take pictures of the event and include them, along with a description of the event, in a notebook. Acting out events ensures that your child will remember the information for quite some time.

I've found that my boys enjoy lots of varied activity. They don't want to sit down and complete worksheets every day. Try adding in these and any other activities you can think of to turn their schoolwork into a game and you will face much less resistance from your sons while homeschooling.

Teaching Boys

Top Ten Ways to Engage Young Sons

Traditional schools can be torturous for young boys. They are forced to sit still for long periods, to be quiet, to do lots of worksheets, etc. The typical American classroom is not the ideal learning environment for our sons, especially in the early grades.

With that in mind, we don't need to replicate a "regular" school when homeschooling boys. We need to harness the incredible energy of our boys and channel it in a way that makes learning fun.

Try these top ten ways to engage your sons' minds and help them want to learn.

1. **Let them move** - Play a variety of music and let them dance. Their dancing may look more like running and chasing, but it lets the wiggles out so they can concentrate again. Anything you can do to have regular breaks that incorporate movement is good. Allow them to run laps or do jumping jacks between subjects.

Laughing and giggling are also good releases. Tell jokes, make faces, and be silly.

2. Make it a game - Let them write on white boards instead of paper and teach them jingles with hand motions and dance moves. Anything you can do to make it fun will work.

3. Let them choose what to do next - Boys love being in charge and directing part of their day, so give them two subjects from which to choose. Be flexible. If you are planning to tackle a topic and your boys start chanting that they want to dance or if they are bursting with energy, be willing to shelve your own agenda momentarily. After their wiggle break, they will have an easier time focusing on what you say.

> *We don't need to replicate a "regular" school when homeschooling boys.*

4. Give them hands-on activities - Boys love to build, cut, and create anything to get their hands dirty. Build block cities, create paper mache and clay exploding volcanoes, dig in the dirt to uncover archaeological artifacts, or learn about measurements by baking. Your boys will never want to stop learning when you present it in this manner.

5. Give them rewards - Give your boys something to look forward to, especially when they are tackling a task that isn't a favorite, such as writing, sitting, listening, or being quiet. Have a visible candy basket on hand for motivation. Let them put stickers on the top of their pages when they do a good job. It is always extra fun when you have a treat such as circus peanuts to toss into their open mouths when they give a correct answer.

6. Throw away the worksheets - Most boys take longer to master writing skills. Since written work doesn't come as easily for boys, many will balk as soon as they see you pull out a worksheet. Let them do most of their answers orally when they are young. Let them dictate the answers to you while you write them down.

Boys usually prefer filling in notebooks or doing longer assignments rather than worksheets. Buy them nice, leather-bound journals to create something lasting, and their attitudes will change. Let them draw pictures and dictate their experiences to you to make journals. They can dictate stories, poems, or songs they have created. These items will become treasured keepsakes.

7. Create healthy competition - Ask questions, allowing your kids to go back and forth giving answers. Keep track of correct answers on a white board like a quiz show with lots of yelling and clapping when they give the right answers. Boys love to see who can get done first or who can do something the best.

Tailor these competitions so that younger siblings have an opportunity to compete on their own level. Use a timer so your son can see how quickly he can complete a task competing against himself.

8. Allow experimentation - Don't simply read the information from a book – allow your son to discover it for himself. Do an experiment first, and then read about it. Your sons will listen more closely when they have a visual picture in their minds.

Show them how colors mix and change with water and food coloring, let them see what sinks and floats in the bathtub, and let them plant seeds and watch them grow, etc. The messier these experiments are, the more they will enjoy and remember them.

9. Play music to make learning stick - Riding in the car is a great learning opportunity. Listen to books on tape, science facts put to silly music, or Bible verses put to song; the possibilities are endless. You will find that running errands is more pleasant when your son's mind is engaged. Squabbles don't normally take place unless kids are bored. Take advantage of car time!

10. Let them outside - Boys have a ton of energy, and they need to burn some of that every day. Fresh air and exercise will do wonders for them. Even in the winter, they need time outdoors for undirected play. Bundle them up and send them outside with a sled and a shovel. You will be amazed at what they discover to entertain themselves.

Our sons are intelligent, motivated, and bursting with energy, which is exactly how God made them. Reach them where they are, direct their energy, and you will be amazed at how quickly they learn. Before long, your sons will be asking why they aren't doing school on Saturdays.

The Best Way to Learn

We've probably all heard the saying "You can lead a horse to water but you can't make him drink." Learning is a lot like that. You can try to force learning on your child – but the best learning definitely comes when it's about something that interests your child.

I've certainly found that to be true for my sons. We'll be reading something together and suddenly it sparks a question in one of my boys. We Google the answer and that can lead to another question and another… and the next thing you know, we're laughing, their eyes are sparkling, and we're all learning.

The learning that happens in this way is spontaneous, it is always off plan, and it is effortless.

I used to think that when my boys had a question that wasn't related to what I was teaching them that they were trying to take me down a rabbit trail… that it was a mere distraction. I now know that it is a spark of curiosity about something has been lit in them. When this happens, I need to be willing to drop whatever I'm doing and fan their desire to learn into a flame.

3 Top Tools for Learning:

1. The Internet – Keep a Kindle, an iPad, a cell phone, or some other device nearby while learning is taking place so that it can easily be consulted when the spark of curiosity hits. I have a Nook that I keep in our living room. When my boys ask me a question for which I don't know the answer, I say, "I don't know. Let me consult my brain." We Google the answer and discuss whatever it is about which they're curious.

2. Flexibility – We need to have a willingness to be flexible. Be ready to pounce on any little spark of curiosity and dive into it. We were reading about Thomas Edison one day when my youngest son asked, "So… who invented the toilet?" That led to an interesting study on the history of toilets. My boys were thrilled to learn that the plumber who popularized the flush toilet was named Thomas Crapper. That was the thrill of our day for sure! And I doubt that either I or my boys will ever forget that little tidbit of trivia.

3. Time – I'm famous for being a planner and being in a rush. I love to use lists and I love to check things off of those lists. These traits are NOT helpful for spontaneous learning. I need to continually remind myself that it's much more important to let my boys dive deep into things which interest them than it is for them to get everything checked off of their list.

While teaching your boys, try to keep in mind the best way to learn and determine to take advantage of these opportunities whenever they present themselves. The more you are willing to explore your son's passions with him, the more inquisitive your son will become.

What To Do When Your Child Hits a Wall

If your children are anything like mine, you've probably had periods of time when one of them becomes frustrated with a particular subject. I remember when my youngest son was struggling with reading. His older brother was reading **The Chronicles of Narnia**[36] in Second Grade; so, I was completely unprepared when this son didn't take to reading right away. He was stuck on **Amelia Bedelia**[37] and **Mr. Putter and Tabby**[38] level books for way longer than I ever dreamed he would be.

It takes each child different amounts of time to master a subject. When things are going along smoothly and all of a sudden your child balks, like they're hitting a wall, what is the best way to proceed?

---

[36] The Chronicles of Narnia by C. S. Lewis
[37] Amelia Bedelia by Peggy Parish
[38] Mr. Putter and Tabby series by Cynthia Rylant

Here are some tips for when your child hits a wall:

1. Be patient – Getting frustrated with your child will only increase the frustration that they are already feeling. Try to remain calm as you explain things. Be encouraging.

My son who struggled with reading is now a voracious reader. He has a love for reading that I might have destroyed if I had pushed him to read at a higher level than what he could handle at the time. We need to remember that grade levels are artificial constructs created by administrators in modern school systems and let our children move forward as quickly or as slowly as is best for them.

2. Don't take it personally – The fact that your child is struggling is not a reflection on you and it doesn't mean that you are a failure as a teacher. Keep in mind, however, that you may need to change your teaching methods or curriculum for your child to be able to relate to it better. Don't feel like you're wasting money if you switch to new material. You can always sell your unwanted items on Ebay!

3. **Get someone else involved** – Sometimes, just getting your husband or a grandparent to explain a topic to your child is enough. This gives him a chance to hear instructions in a slightly different way. If your child is really struggling, you may need to hire a professional tutor who can better explain things to your child. This is especially true if the topic with which your child is having difficulty is also a tricky one for you.

4. Take a step backwards – I've found that when my boys hit a wall, it is beneficial to go backwards to material that is easy for them. This helps to build their confidence tremendously. After a few days of doing the easier work, try the harder material again and see how they do. Often, they will be able to crash right through that pesky wall and continue moving forward.

Schools expect students to learn the same material at the same rate. One of the advantages that homeschoolers have is that we can give our children the freedom to learn at their own pace. If we allow our children to learn things when they are ready rather than pushing them to learn before they are ready, then they will catch up and go well beyond where they would have gone if we had pushed them faster than they are comfortable.

> *Our children have the freedom to learn at their own pace.*

Another thing to keep in mind is that all kids have strengths and weaknesses. They were not created out of cookie cutter molds, as much as schools would like that think that they are. They will not all master every subject to the same degree. Some of our children will go on to become great mathematicians. Some of them will be brilliant scientists. Still others will write beautiful poetry and literature. Watch your children to see where they excel and feed their passions and their strengths.

Yes, all students need at least some mastery of reading, writing, and arithmetic; however, not all students have the desire or the ability to master calculus. Watch your child to determine how he is wired, what he is interested in, what methods of learning appeal to him, what time of day he learns best, etc.

As homeschoolers we have so much flexibility to teach our children in a manner that will be best for their individual needs. Let's take advantage of that flexibility and rearrange our homeschools to cater to the unique children that God has entrusted into our care.

Evaluate Student Learning

Taking time to evaluate student learning is important. Through the year, it is important to determine where your child's strong and weak points lie. Identifying strengths and areas of interest is important because that will help you to know the types of things your son may be interested in pursuing and learning more about in the coming year. Identifying weaknesses is important so that you can spend more time instructing your son in those subjects to try to help him catch up to where he should be.

If your child is weak in a certain area, that may be an indication that you should consider switching to a different curriculum for that subject. Sometimes just having things approached from a different angle will give your son enough stimulation for him to want to try harder in that subject.

Homeschooling parents usually have a much better idea of what their children know and what they struggle with than do parents whose children attend school outside of the home. As you're teaching your child, it's pretty easy to tell when they've grasped a subject and when you need to continue to work with him before moving on.

Homeschooled children aren't always getting graded, however, so it's hard to prove to grandparents and the rest of the outside world that our children are doing well compared to their schooled peers.

Some homeschoolers turn to standardized testing in order to prove that their children are learning and are on par with other students. This isn't necessarily an approach I would recommend. For one thing, schools spend an inordinate amount of their time and resources preparing their children specifically to take these tests.

Because schools spend so much time preparing their students to take standardized tests, some of them have been forced to cut back or even eliminate recess for young children, and other electives for high schoolers. Teachers find they can't have discussions about current events in the classroom because that material will not appear on the tests. Some teachers have even eliminated entire subject areas such as science if the test will only cover language arts and math.

Entire years are devoted to "studying for the test" in schoolrooms. This can make it hard and undesirable to compare your children to if you are not using this same approach at home. Of course, the test results of most homeschooled children compare favorably to children who have been sent to school – so you will need to decide for yourself if this is an approach you want to take.

Homeschoolers run the risk of being overly concerned with how their children score on these tests and making the same mistakes as have the schools. There are ways to teach your children similar information to what kids in schools are learning in each grade without taking having to study for standardized tests. If this is important to you, I would instead recommend having a list of skills and information that are taught for each grade and using that.

Remember, however, that not all schools teach the same things – and you won't cover everything exactly the same as your local school... and that's a good thing. There are things being taught in schools these days that make me sad. Character education is all but forgotten in the public schools... and parents don't have time to teach any life skills to their kids because they're too busy helping them finish hours of homework every night.

> *Entire years are devoted to "studying for the test" in schoolrooms.*

And one of the huge advantages of homeschooling is that we're able to teach our kids material when they're ready rather than according to some arbitrary timetable made up by a committee that doesn't know anything about your child.

So take heart! Remember the reasons you wanted to homeschool – it wasn't because you wanted to duplicate your local public school. Stay true to your values and your sons will grow up with integrity and with plenty of learning accomplished as well.

Giving Your Children an Exemplary Education

Sometimes homeschoolers feel that they should copy the educational model of various public schools which are around them. They buy desks for each of their children, line them up in a row, set up rigid schedules… some even ring bells to go from subject to subject.

Homeschoolers should never feel that they need to try to "keep up" with the public schools in their area. The homeschool model of education is far superior to that found in most brick and mortar schools.

In 1995, Stetson University, Osceola Public School District, and Disney Development Corporation joined forces to try to develop what would be considered an exemplary" school for kindergarten through grade twelve. Millions of dollars were spent bringing together the greatest educational minds in the country to develop what could be considered the brightest and best school system in the country.

You may or may not be shocked at what they discovered, which included the following:

- Classes should be small and should contain children of a variety of ages.

- Various subjects should be taught together.

- Flexible scheduling should be employed to promote maximum learning when it is best for the child.

- Learning areas should be filled with sofas and chairs rather than desks lined in a row.

- Classrooms should be active, sometimes noisy environments.

The exemplary educational model they came up with sounds exactly like the homeschooling model. Millions of dollars were spent to discover that what homeschoolers are doing works – and it educates our children excellently.

As homeschoolers, we sometimes feel pressured by friends and family to mould our homeschools around the ideals of the local school system. This is unfortunate since their model of education doesn't work as well! We should feel comfortable allowing our children to experience very different school days than do their schooled peers. We should not feel pressured to look more like the brick and mortar school down the street.

Another important point that was discovered from their research was that a personalized learning plan should be developed for each student – not just for the learning disabled or the gifted. As homeschoolers, we need to remember this for our children as well. Instead of blindly following some curriculum or company's advice for our children, we need to make sure we have an individualized plan for each of our children.

> *Millions of dollars were spent to discover that what homeschoolers are doing works – and it educates our children excellently.*

Some useful questions when developing this type of personalized learning plan are the following:

- Where is the child at in each subject?
- With what skills does he struggle?
- What are his strengths?
- Where does he want to go?
- In what is he most interested?
- Consider the child's preferred method of learning – in which way will he best retain the information?
- What does the child want to do in life and how can he get there?
- What subjects are necessary if this child decides to pursue his dream career?
- How can we best guide him?

Our children are all different and we need to develop individualized learning plans for each of them, keeping their particular interests and strengths in mind.

As homeschoolers, we have the freedom and ability to implement the most exemplary model of education which has been found for teaching children. Spending thousands of dollars per student isn't what is necessary for the proper education of our children. What is important is that their individualized needs are taken into account on a daily basis.

Our homeschools, which are furnished with comfortable couches and which are filled with the sound of laughter and conversation, are doing a great job of educating our children. We need to stop second guessing ourselves. The homeschooling model has been proven to work well. Be encouraged!

Choosing Good Books

Have you ever started reading a book with your children only to discover that it contains content which is objectionable? I've started reading several books in which I've had to skip over or change an occasional word. Some books contain themes with which we don't agree, excessive cursing, descriptions of suicide, drug and alcohol abuse, or other things I don't feel my boys are ready to handle at this point in their lives. If I'm reading the book aloud, I've been known to close it and tell my boys that we aren't going to finish that one because it has bad stuff in it.

That's all well and good if you're reading the book aloud. But how do you know the book is any good when you hand it to your children to read on their own? At this age, my boys read enough books on their own that I couldn't possible pre-read everything in advance to check for good content.

I rely on several different sources to know whether or not a book is one I feel comfortable handing to my child:

1. ***Read for the Heart*** [39] **by Sarah Clarkson** – I love this book. Sarah has personally read each of the books she recommends and she includes a short synopsis for each of them. She also identifies any mature themes or issues for which parents should be aware. We have chosen lots of great books using this resource.

2. ***Honey for a Child's Heart*** [40] **by Gladys Hunt** – This book is an oldie but a goodie. Similar to the above book, this book contains recommendations for many quality children's books.

3. **Recommendations from Friends with Similar Convictions** – There are so many books out there and many of them aren't included in either of the above books. Ask other homeschoolers to keep a list of books their family has enjoyed and you can do the same for them. Swap these lists to get some great book recommendations. Be sure the people you ask have similar convictions to yourself or you may be surprised by some of their selections.

4. **Classics** – Not all classics are appropriate for children. I was going to have my 11-year-old read ***Fahrenheit 451*** [41] by Ray Bradbury this year and was shocked when I started pre-reading it. The themes were way too mature for him and the language contained more cursing than I remembered from when I read this book in my school days. Also, if you've ever read ***East of Eden*** [42] by John Steinbeck or ***Madame Bovary*** [43] by Gustave

---

[39] Read for the Heart by Sarah Clarkson
[40] Honey for a Child's Heart by Gladys Hunt
[41] Fahrenheit 451 by Ray Bradbury
[42] East of Eden by John Steinbeck
[43] Madame Bovary by Gustave Flaubert

Flaubert, you'll know that just because it's considered a classic doesn't mean you want your child to read it.

One of the great things about classics is that you can usually find ample information about these books on the internet. Some of the sites I use for finding out more about these materials are: eNotes[44], Bookrags[45], Sparknotes[46], and Progeny Press[47].

5. Book Publishers – Find book publishers that you trust and look through their catalogs to find good reading suggestions. I love looking at Veritas Press [48] for book ideas. I do think their suggestions are quite advanced by grade, however, and I usually choose selections which are a grade or two lower than what they suggest. I also love Lamplighter Books.[49]

6. **Your Child's Internal Sensor** – Sometimes your child will choose a book that he wants to read. You may not be able to do more than read the front and back flap before you have to make a decision. At that point, you need to trust that your child has internalized what you've taught him. Teach him that if he encounters material which he feels is inappropriate to put the book down.

We need to make a good effort to present descent, quality material for our children to read. At some point, however, they need to start making these decisions for themselves. Depending on your child's age and maturity, of course, this is another

---

[44] http://www.enotes.com/
[45] http://www.bookrags.com/
[46] http://www.sparknotes.com/
[47] http://stores.progenypress.com/
[48] https://www.veritaspress.com/
[49] http://lamplighter.net/c/

method for helping him to develop his own ability to discern good reading material.

Reading is an excellent way for our children to learn about the world around them. Once our kids begin reading large quantities of books on their own, however, it can be difficult to know whether or not the books they are reading are filled with quality material. Using the above methods will help to ensure that they are not only reading books but that they are choosing good books on their own as well.

Reading Living Books vs Textbooks

I recently checked out a book from the library called ***Invitation to the Classics*** [50] by Louise Cowan and Os Guinness. As I was looking through the book, it brought to mind different excerpts I had been assigned to read from English textbooks through the years as part of my public school education.

Unfortunately, it also made me realize how few actual BOOKS we read for class. I only remember reading one full book a year in 7th and 8th grade, one of which was ***Where the Red Fern Grows*** [51] ... and that was about it. And in high school we only had to read 2 or 3 books each year. The rest of the time we read excerpts from textbooks.

When we started our homeschool journey, I had my boys read textbook readers because that's the method of learning that was familiar to me. At some point, however, I heard the terms "classical education" and "living books" and was intrigued.

---

[50] Invitation to the Classics by Louise Cowan and Os Guinness
[51] Where the Red Fern Grows by Wilson Rawls

Living books are defined by Charlotte Mason as *"whole books, firsthand sources, classics, books that display imagination, originality, and those having the 'human touch.'"* The thought of having my children learn by reading real books was appealing to me. It was also scary to think that I wouldn't be following a "professional's" educational standards (i.e., teacher's manuals.)

So I started our homeschool experience using textbooks and teacher's manuals and felt safe. That is, until my sons started to complain about how they didn't like to read. They had always LOVED it when I read to them so I was shocked to think that they might not grow up to be readers themselves.

When my oldest son found a book he enjoyed reading on his own and devoured it, but still complained about the reading I was making him do for schoolwork, I knew something needed to change.

> *Reading living books transformed our homeschool experience.*

Once I switched my boys to reading real books, they started to enjoy reading so much more. They begged to read additional chapters every day. They never wanted to continue reading when we were using textbooks – and they were reading LESS pages in the textbooks. Reading living books transformed our homeschool experience.

I highly recommend throwing out some of the textbooks and picking up some regular books instead. We did continue to use a textbook for math – but that was all. I can't tell you how much more my boys started to enjoying school since we made the switch! And guess which subject they always want to start with each morning. You guess it – reading!

Take a leap, give reading real books a try, and reap the rewards.

Make Your Own Homeschool Preschool Curriculum

Have you thought about homeschooling your child – but aren't sure you have what it takes to persevere? Homeschooling during the preschool ages is a great way to try everything out and see if it's going to work for your family.

Following a homeschool preschool children has many side benefits. It gives you something constructive to do during those long daytime hours while your husband is at work. And it will help you bond with your children in a way that nothing else will. Watching your preschooler learn and grow is a wonderful experience – and one that you and your child will both enjoy.

You can purchase a great homeschool preschool curriculum that is all ready to go, if that's what you're interested in doing. Or, you can come up with activities on your own. When I first started doing preschool activities with our boys, I came up with learning activities for them by searching the internet. This does take a lot of extra planning time; however.

Later on, we worked through the Bob Jones 3-year-old preschool program[52] and also the Bob Jones 4-year-old preschool program[53]. We enjoyed these programs and they saved me a bunch of time trying to figure out what to do next!

Below is a list of fun preschool activities for you to try with your child.

Preschool Fine Motor Skills:

- Let your children play with pattern blocks. See what kinds of patterns they can come up with on their own. Make a pattern and let them try to copy it. This is lots of fun for little ones.

- Have two bowls, one empty and one filled with cotton balls. Give your child a pair of kitchen tongs. Let him use the tongs to pick up the cotton balls and transfer them from one bowl to the other. Depending on the age of your child, he may need to use two hands to operate the tongs at first. It takes more coordination than you may realize to grip and release the tongs.

- Give your children some animal crackers, a can of frosting, and a plastic knife. Let them frost their crackers and eat them. This is a huge hit with kids of all ages. For a healthier alternative, let your children spread peanut butter on a piece of toast.

---

[52] Bob Jones Pathways for Preschool
[53] Bob Jones Footsteps for Fours

- Buy a large whiteboard and some dry erase markers for your child and let him go to town.

- Let your children finger paint with whipped cream and construction paper. This is another huge hit with kids – and it won't hurt them if they're still at the age where they put things in their mouth. You can even use food coloring to give them different colors of "paint". It's easier to clean up, though, if you leave the whipped cream white and let them paint snow pictures.

- Give your child markers, crayons, pencils, etc. and let him scribble to his heart's content. This helps with developing hand-eye coordination. You can make rudimentary dot-to-dot pictures for him to follow, if you'd like. When your child is young and first starts working with paper and writing utensils, I'd recommend taping his paper to the table. He will have enough things to concentrate on without having to try to hold down his paper at the same time.

- Give your child lace-up cards to play with.

- Give your child different types of blocks to play with. Let him stack them, make roads for his car with them… however he'd like to play with them. Kids have more active imaginations than we do so follow his lead.

- Lincoln logs are another fun activity – especially when dad can also be involved. Children will be delighted to see the wonderful creations that they can make together with their fathers.

- Puzzles are a great way to help preschoolers develop their fine motor skills. Have a variety of puzzles on hand because that will be more visually interesting to your child.

- Give your child a piece of scrap paper and a pair of scissors and let him fringe the paper. This is the first step in helping him learn to cut. After he masters this skill, draw a thick outline of a square or circle on a piece of paper and have him practice cutting on the lines.

- Paper dolls are a fun activity for more advanced preschoolers.

- Give your child a set of beads that he can practice lacing onto the string.

- Give your child some Playdoh, a rolling pin, and some cookie cutters and let him play.

More Preschool Fun:

- Draw a rainbow on a large piece of paper. Give your child a bowl of Fruit Loops cereal and let him match the cereal pieces to the right colors on the rainbow.

- Read to your children. When they are very little, they might not want to sit still through an entire picture book. But the more you read to them, the longer they will want you to read to them. This is a wonderful way for them to develop a longer attention span, to develop their speech and grammar abilities, and many other valuable skills.

- Have old clothes in a box and let your child play dress-up. Try having him act out stories or nursery rhymes as you read him, such as ***The Three Little Bears*** or ***Little Miss Muffet***.

- Give your children empty boxes and let them climb in them, store toys in them, draw on them, make teepees out of them, or do whatever else they'd like to do with them. As your children get older, you can also let them cut up the boxes to make other creations from their own imaginations.

- Let your child sample different types of fruits and vegetables than the ones you normally buy. Make it a special event so that he will be thrilled to try an exotic fruit or vegetable. Be sure to let your child help prepare the food as there is so much learning that can be done in the kitchen helping Mommy.

- Pull a variety of spices out of your spice cupboard, have your child close his eyes, and let him smell them one at a time. You will be amazed at how this simple activity will thrill your child. See if he can identify the spices the third or fourth time around.

- Put a 2×4 on the floor and let your child try to walk across it without falling off. This is a great activity for developing his gross motor skills.

- Print off pictures of events from a story and let your child put the pictures in the right order. This is called Sequencing.

- Clap or slap a rhythm on your legs and let your child try to copy the same rhythm.

- Label common objects around your house to help your child become familiar with some words.

- A fun science experiment is to fill a small glass with water and another glass with milk. Put a straw in both glasses. Let your child blow into each glass and see what happens. Be sure to have towels handy for this one!

- Take a walk with your child. The object with this one isn't to see how far and how fast you can go. Slow down, observe objects around you, and listen to what your child has to say. Let your child carry a bag with him to collect rocks, leaves, and whatever else catches his eye.

- Let your child make crowns, Indian hats, etc and dance around the house. Try making costumes to match characters in books that you are reading (i.e., make rabbit ears when reading Peter Rabbit.)

- Let your child dictate stories to you and you can write them down in a book or journal for him. Also, let him illustrate the stories. These creations make wonderful keepsakes and/or gifts for grandparents.

- Give your child sidewalk chalk and let him doodle all over the driveway.

- Take field trips with your child. Take him to the zoo, a children's museum, plays and concerts which are geared for younger children, etc. Let him experience the world around him.

This is just a sampling of some of the fun activities that you can do as part of your homeschool preschool experience. The more time you spend with your child, the more you will get to know where his individual interests and talents lie… and you can explore those in more depth with him.

At this age, the main thing is for your child to enjoy learning and to build your relationship with him. Relax, have fun with your child, and watch him blossom.

If you'd like to see even more fun preschool activities, you'll want to check out my **Learn & Grow: Hands-on Lessons for Active Preschoolers**.

Making Math Marvelous

Teaching Math Creatively

One of my sons hates math. Period. Every day when it's time to do our math, his face gets sullen and he digs in his heels. He would rather do any other subject in the world than math. But, unfortunately for him, math is one of those subjects that most families do every day.

This same son used to enjoy math when he was younger. Back in the days when we would use counters to add and subtract, he enjoyed math. When we used pattern blocks and an abacus, he loved math. But once he got to about 5th grade and was having to complete math worksheets, he started to hate math.

Both of my sons prefer hands-on learning. Neither of them is the type of child who wants to sit at the table and write anything, let alone to fill in math worksheets every day. Worksheets are easier for the teacher but most students find them to be tedious.

Because of this, we've had to come up with different ways to supplement my son's math to make it more enjoyable.

Try these Tips for Teaching Math Creatively:

1. Jump Around – One thing we've done is to jump around in our math book. The math books we use contain different chapters which concentrate on themes, such as multiplication in one chapter and geometry in the next.

My son doesn't dislike all math. In fact, he enjoys the chapters in his book which focus on anything other than adding, subtracting, multiplying and dividing. So instead of making him complete two pages which concentrate on the same subject and caused great angst, I started to give him one page to do with regular arithmetic and one page which focused on something else.

If you look in your child's math book, you'll see that there are lots of other activities encompassed in math, such as Roman numerals, logic, geometry, fractions, measurement, and time. If your math curriculum also focuses mainly on one topic per lesson, try combining lessons to give your child more variety. This has helped my son to be able to almost enjoy math… although he wouldn't yet admit it!

2. Computer Math – Another idea we've tried is letting the boys use a computer math game as a supplement to their math book. There are lots of programs out there, depending on your child's grade level. Jumpstart[54] and multiplication.com[55] are free websites which allow your child to play games while practicing their math skills.

---

[54] http://www.jumpstart.com/
[55] http://www.multiplication.com/games/all-games

You may also want to check out the software which is available from Encore. They produce the Elementary Advantage, Middle School Advantage, and High School Advantage computer software[56]. We have found their products to be fun and the boys pick up a lot of information without realizing they are learning.

3. Get Dad Involved – Another idea which we've had success with on occasion was to leave math until dad got home at night. There is something about Dads and math which go together. When I start to encounter extra resistance from my boys with math (or any other subject, for that matter), we start having the boys work on it with my husband at night. This works on a couple of different levels.

First, my husband is able to explain things to our boys in a way that they more readily understand. They communicate using man language. It sounds like the same explanation to me; but, somehow when the words are coming out of their father's mouth, it is more understandable to them.

Second, the boys would rather be doing anything other than math with their dad when he gets home from work. This encourages them to try harder to complete their math during the day, with the rest of their subjects, so that they can have more free time with dad when he gets home.

4. Math War – Try getting out a couple decks of cards and playing war with the kids. If your child is young, you can play the regular game of war, where each player flips over one card at

---

[56] http://www.encore.com/

a time and whoever has the largest card captures the other players' cards.

> *Somehow, when the words are coming out of their father's mouth, it is more understandable to them.*

If your child is older, you can give the game a twist. Instead of merely flipping over one card per player, flip over two per player. Everyone then either needs to add, subtract, multiply, or divide their cards to determine the winner. This game is fast paced and adds a lot of fun to what would otherwise be drudgery to some kids.

5. Remove the Writing – Some kids hate to write anything down. The mere act of writing causes them to go into an anxiety attack. If you remove the writing from math, this will help you to know if it's really math that they dislike or if it's the writing that they dislike. Boys, especially, can have a tendency to lag behind with their writing skills.

If you act as a scribe for your child, writing down his answers, showing all of the work, that is enough for some kids to transform their math into a positive experience. Be sure that if you try this method, you require your child to tell you exactly what to write down. Try not to lead him through solving the problems. You want to be sure they are doing all of the thinking and you are merely being their hands.

Try thinking out of the box when it comes to math. Any time you can get your kids DOING something versus simply sitting and writing, you'll find that their enjoyment as well as the amount of learning they accomplish will go way up.

6 Ways to Get Boys to Consume the Classics

When I was in 9th grade, my English teacher, Mrs. Rensch, attempted to have our class read Romeo and Juliet out loud. She assigned parts to some of the stronger readers in the class and we gave it a go.

It didn't take very long for her to realize that we weren't getting anything out of it. We didn't have any idea how to read Shakespeare properly and we were turning it into a dry, agonizing experience. Her attempt to enlighten us about the humor in the literature was completely lost on us.

After a few days, she had us close our books and put our heads down on our desks. Mrs. Rensch explained that Shakespeare's works weren't initially meant to be read – but to be watched and heard. She put on a record (yes, a record – I know that dates me) of Romeo and Juliet and had us listen to the play as it was performed by experienced Shakespearean actors.

Suddenly, the words made sense. It wasn't merely read – it was performed. And lo and behold, there actually were funny parts!

After we finished listening to the play, she brought in a TV and we watched the performance as well. We got so much more out of it by her teaching methods than if we had merely read the play as a class – or even worse, tried reading it silently to ourselves.

If you've been trying to get your sons to read classic literature and it isn't going very well, there are some different methods that you can try.

Here are 6 Ways to Get Boys to Consume the Classics:

1. **Choose Wisely** – Some classics are just plain boring. Seriously. I LOVE to read – but some of the books are so hard to get through that it can feel like you need to plow through them with a shovel versus being able to enjoy them and get something out of them. I remember having to read a novel by Henry James in high school and struggling terribly with it.

> **Some classics are just plain boring. Seriously.**

The sentences were as long as normal paragraphs and the paragraphs went on for pages! The only way I made it through that book was to read it out loud to myself. Hearing the words helped me to follow along better than by merely reading them in my head. But even then, I don't even remember the title of that book to this day, not to mention learning anything from reading it.

On the other hand, I fondly remember reading exciting classic books such as **Les Miserables**[57], **The Count of Monte Cristo**[58], and **1984**[59]. Boys (and many girls) are going to have a much easier time reading a book with plenty of action versus a book where the author goes on for page after page describing a tea towel or talking about feelings.

2. Read them Aloud – Quite often, classic books are ones I will choose as read aloud options. This helps me to be able to discuss them more fully with my boys while we are reading them… and to gauge whether or not they are getting anything out of the book.

3. Audio books – Sometimes the wording and/or phrasing in classic books can be difficult to comprehend. If heard read by a trained voice actor, however, they are quite delightful. Try having your son listen to an audio book while following along with his own copy. This will help him to get much more out of the experience than merely reading the book.

You can find lots of audio books at your local library. Also, there are many FREE audio books, especially of classic works, which you can download from various sites such as Open Culture[60].

4. Dramatized versions – There are also times when hearing a dramatized version of the book will teach your son what you want him to learn much more vividly. There are some amazing

---

[57] Les Misearables by Victor Hugo
[58] The Count of Monte Cristo by Alexandre Dumas
[59] 1984 by George Orwell
[60] http://www.openculture.com/

dramatized books out there. We recently purchased a couple of dramatized G.A. Henty books that are fantastic called ***In Freedom's Cause*** [61] and ***Under Drake's Flag*** [62].

5. Abridged versions – Depending on the age of your child and the purpose behind your wanting him to read a classic work, your son may be able to get just as much if not more out of reading an abridged version of a book. When my boys were younger, we enjoyed reading classics from the ***Classic Starts Series*** [63].

6. Movies – There are some amazing movies based on classic works. Sometimes, if your son is struggling to get through a book, knowing that he can watch the movie when he's done will help him to continue plodding through. Sometimes, there is just as much value from merely watching the movie rather than reading the book at all. **Whenever possible, I do try to have my boys read the book BEFORE they watch the movie.**

When choosing which movies to watch, be sure to do your research. Some movies veer quite far away from the book on which they're based. Unless we have a trusted recommendation to go by, I usually search for the oldest movie I can find and view that one. The older movies tend to follow the books more closely and to include direct quotes from the books.

The way we approach classic works will determine whether our sons will enjoy them or whether they will avoid them like the plague. Whether or not your son is an avid reader there are ways to help him enjoy classic works as much as he enjoys

---

[61] In Freedom's Cause audio drama by Heirloom Audio Productions
[62] Under Drake's Flag audio drama by Heirloom Audio Productions
[63] Classic Starts series by various authors

reading ***The Chronicles of Narnia*** [64] and ***The Lord of the Rings*** [65]. By the way, those are great classics to start your son with if he hasn't read them, yet!

---

[64] The Chronicles of Narnia by C. S. Lewis
[65] The Lord of the Rings by J. R. R. Tolkien

Homeschool Record Keeping

I'm fortunate to live in a state where the homeschool requirements are quite lenient. Homeschoolers where I live aren't required to report to the local school district, to get curriculum approved by the powers that be, or to get kids tested on a regular basis. We are also not required to keep records of what the kids accomplish from year to year – at least not in the early grades.

Homeschool record keeping is still a good idea, however. It isn't something I did when we first started homeschooling; but, it is something I kept meaning to go back and catch up on for my boys. In fact, every year that I wasn't keeping records, I made a resolution to go back and compile all of the things they had accomplished for our own satisfaction.

My boys have done lots of interesting activities that I didn't want to forget. So one year, several years into homeschooling, I finally bit the bullet and sat down to create a record book for my boys' school career thus far.

First, I created a record for what we were doing that year. That was obviously the easiest place to start because all the subjects that we were currently doing were fresh in my mind. I added a picture of that child from the current year to help me see how much they were maturing from year to year.

Then I listed out each subject along with the specific materials we were using. I broke the year into two semesters and gave grades as well. In the elementary years, we didn't move on with material until my boys were doing A-level work. As they got older, however, we kept track of grades more in line with the way they do in schools.

Subject	Materials	Semester 1	Semester 2
Devotions	Keys for Kids	A	A
Bible	Apologia Apologetics – Who am I? And What am I Doing Here?	A	A
Awana	Truth & Training – Ultimate Challenge Book 3	A	A
Reading	Various books from library	A	A
Spelling	Downloaded lists from internet	A	A
Math	Bob Jones Math 5	A	A
English	Bob Jones English 5	A	A
Geography	Mapping the World by Heart	A	A

Next, I added a list of the books that I had read out loud to my boys that year. We always start our day with me reading aloud to the boys. We've found that to be a wonderful way to ease into our school day. After that, I listed all the books that my child had read on their own that year. I also listed all of the audio books they had listened to.

Some years I have been better at keeping a book list than others. I think that when you keep track of these, you'll be amazed at how many books your child will have read throughout the year.

Finally, I listed out the extracurricular activities and field trips in which each child had participated. Be sure to include family activities, day trips, and vacations in this list!

Once you get all of this recorded for your current year, I would recommend going back to the previous year and so on until you get as much as you can remember recorded for each year. Fortunately, I had kept book lists for some of my sons' earliest years of homeschooling. I also used photos that I had taken to trigger my memory for past field trips and extracurricular activities.

I put our school records into a three ring binder, placing each page inside a plastic sheet protector for convenience and so that they will wear well. I also recommend that you save these records in a computer file so that they can be easily updated and reprinted as you remember more and more.

Record keeping is the type of chore that some homeschool moms dread; but, once you get started, you may find yourself pleasantly surprised. Creating these records brings back some fond memories and they will be a keepsake for you and your children for years to come.

Homeschool High School Record Keeping

I remember how shocked I was the first year that I was homeschooling a high school student. I couldn't believe how quickly we had arrived at this phase of our lives. The time really does go by quickly. Not each individual day, necessarily – but the months and the years fly by. Treasure this time, parents!

The summer before my oldest son's freshman year, I spent lots of time researching what types of homeschool high school record keeping we needed to do at that phase of my son's life.

Fortunately, the prior spring I had the privilege of taking several workshops by Lee Binz, author of several books who blogs at TheHomeScholar.com[66]. Lee has two sons who she homeschooled through high school. These sons both received full scholarships from the college of their choice! So Lee knows what she's talking about when it comes to homeschool record keeping. I gleaned some helpful information from listening to Lee – information which made me feel much more comfortable about that stage of homeschooling!

---

[66] www.thehomescholar.com

Things you should keep for each year you homeschool high school:

1. Items your state law requires you to keep (such as letter of intent to homeschool, etc.)

2. Items which will be helpful for writing course descriptions later (such as book lists, experiences, certificates or awards your child has earned, a copy of the cover and table of contents for textbooks you use – you can probably find copies of these on the internet and print them off)

3. Items colleges may ask to see (such as tests, lab reports, finished written papers)

Lee recommends you make a binder for your child's high school experience. This is what she recommends you put in separate sections of that binder:

- State law requirements
- Transcript
- Course descriptions
- Reading list (books, audio books, video adaptations – include books read for school AND for pleasure)
- Activities and awards
- Work samples

Figuring out credits

Lee said that when she was researching how to determine when to give your child credit for completing a class, she ran across lots of different opinions. Here is what Lee recommends:

- **Count the textbook first** – If your child completes at least 80% of a textbook which states that it is appropriate for high school level work, you should give him 1 credit.

- **College level work** – If your child takes a one semester class at a community college or online, you should give him 1 credit.

NOTE: College classes move faster than high school classes; so, even though a college class is only 1 semester long, it covers the equivalent of a full high school year's work.

- **Electives or Delight Directed Learning** – If your child is reading real books, or having experiences in a specific area of study (such as drama or physical education) then you should count hours to determine credit.

$$120\text{-}180 \text{ hours} = 1 \text{ credit}$$
$$75\text{-}90 \text{ hours} = 1/2 \text{ credit}$$

I'm a planner, so I spent lots of time creating binders for both of my sons. My younger son, Sam, was entering 7th grade the year that my older son was entering the high school years. Since Sam took Algebra I that year, he was completing his first high school class – even though he was only in middle school at the time.

Lee said that we should give our kids credit for any high school work they complete – even if they aren't in high school. Simply put "Early High School Credits" on their transcript for those items.

Lee has some AMAZING resources I highly recommend:

- *The HomeScholar Total Transcript Solution*[67]

- *Setting the Records Straight: How to Craft Homeschool Transcripts and Course Descriptions for College Admission and Scholarships*[68]

- *The HomeScholar Guide to College Admission and Scholarships*[69]

- *Preparing to Homeschool High School: Learn to Homeschool High School with Excellence!*[70]

Lee also has samples of records that she recommends on her website. When my boys were in their early teens, we didn't have a clear idea of what career they would want to pursue after high school. Whether they end up wanting to go to college, into the military, to a trade school, or directly into a job, I want them to have the credentials that they'll need to follow their dreams.

As I learned more about homeschool high school record keeping, I felt much more confident about my boys' options for their future. I hope this information will also help you to feel secure about preparing your own children.

---

[67] The HomeScholar Total Transcript Solution (course) by Lee Binz
[68] Setting the Records Straight by Lee Binz
[69] The HomeScholar Guide to College Admission and Scholarships by Lee Binz
[70] Preparing to Homeschool High School (DVD) by Lee Binz

Homeschool Reading Program

Boys are more likely than girls to say that they hate to read. Boys do get excited about reading, though, if it is approached in the right way and if they are given the right reading material.

As parents, we have the flexibility to design homeschool reading programs which will cater to the needs of our individual children. We also have a head start when teaching our children to read as parental involvement plays a big role in the success of our children's reading ability. The more our children see us reading, the more they will see the value of reading and want to learn to do it themselves.

Here are some specific tips for helping our boys enjoy reading!

- **Audio Books or Dramatized Versions of Books** – Allow your son to listen to audio books. Most libraries have tons of audio books that you can check out. We've also enjoyed listening to dramatized versions of books such as ***Under Drake's Flag***[71] and ***In Freedom's Cause***[72].

- **Boys Book Clubs** – Start a book club just for boys. Try to include dynamic outdoor activities which relate to the book. Think about providing snacks or a pizza party for each boy who successfully completes the book. Sports and adventure genres are great to focus on for these kinds of clubs.

> *Boys get excited about reading if it is approached in the right way*

- **Discuss the Value** – Your sons may not realize how important reading can be for various careers. As part of your homeschool reading program, you will want to discuss different jobs your boys are currently excited about and let them know how important reading can be for those careers. If your sons can grasp the importance of reading, they will be more inclined to want to master the skill.

- **Grab their Attention** – It will be much more productive if you are able to introduce materials into your homeschool reading that will grab their attention rather than forcing them to only read books that you want them to read. Forcing boys to read will not make them lifelong readers – it will turn them into resistance readers.

---

[71] Under Drake's Flag audio drama by Heirloom Audio Productions
[72] In Freedom's Cause audio drama by Heirloom Audio Productions

- **Libraries and Bookstores** – Take your sons to the library or a bookstore. Let them see the vast amount of reading material which is available to them. A great way to get your boys interested in reading is to let them choose the book they will read next.

- **Male Role Models** – Boys who are homeschooled often see their moms reading, but don't necessarily see their dads reading as well. It is important for boys to see men and other boys get excited about reading so that they don't come to the mistaken conclusion that reading is only for women. A great way to get dad involved in the homeschool reading program is for him to read aloud to your boys in the evenings. Try to choose reading material which is slightly more complex than that which your sons are reading on their own.

> *Forcing boys to read will not make them lifelong readers – it will turn them into resistance readers.*

- **Peer Reading** – If you have more than one child, have the older one help the younger one in his reading. Boys look up to their older siblings and love to copy them. Reading with an older brother or sister tends to help the younger boys with their reading skills while helping the older ones to develop better communication and social skills.

- **Read Aloud** – Read aloud to your sons and have them read aloud to you. Unfortunately, once children learn to read on their own, this is a practice that parents often abandon.

Reading aloud to your children is a bridge to more difficult reading that your sons will tackle independently later. It's also a great way for kids to hear complex and correct English language patterns. Reading aloud should be included in every good homeschool reading program.

- **Reading Materials** – Most boys do enjoy reading if they are given the right reading material. Look for the following when choosing reading materials to stimulate your son's desire to read:

    o Books which are based on their own interests or that will help them to gain information that they can share with their friends.

    o Stories they can relate to from their own life experiences.

    o Genres that interest boys usually include fantasy, science-fiction, mysteries and adventure books.

    o Books that jump right into the action and don't spend pages describing the beautiful setting.

    o If you are homeschooling daughters as well as sons, it is important that you are willing to introduce them to some different books as they usually have vastly different reading preferences… especially in the elementary and middle school years.

    o Studies have shown that boys often prefer to read non-fiction material. Some of them are intrigued by fact books such as the ***Guinness Book of World Records*** or the ***Farmer's Almanac***.

- o Let your son subscribe to his own magazine – ones which feature sports, cars, science, or technology are usually favorites among boys.

- o Sometimes boys just want to read for fun. They tend to enjoy books which feature crazy rules or gross details. You'll want to be aware of what your sons are reading in this category, however. You may want to pre-read these types of books to make sure they are appropriate for your family.

- o Comic books can get your boys hooked on reading. If they learn to love reading through comic books, they might be more willing to read their first novel once they become more confident in their skills.

- o Young boys enjoy short books that they can start and finish in one sitting. Once they have learned to enjoy these types of stories, they will be more willing to graduate to longer books.

- **Music** – If your older boys are interested in music, encourage them to read song lyrics and to write song lyrics of their own. They can attempt to write songs about their own school lessons. When lessons are put to music, boys will remember them much longer.

Use these tips to develop your own homeschool reading program and you may never again hear your boys complain about having to read!

13 Benefits of Unit Studies

Have you ever tried using a unit study with your children? If not, you may want to consider giving it a try.

Unit studies are different than the traditional way of homeschooling because rather than studying each subject separately they combine multiple subjects into one set of lessons. Kids are then able to learn all of the various subjects such as reading, history, and science by studying a single topic.

Unit studies encourage students to see an issue as a whole; they see the big picture, not just bits and pieces of it. This is a lot more like learning from real life experience. In fact, good unit studies will incorporate as many real life experiences, such a field trips and science experiments, as possible.

When learning from unit studies, students develop the ability to study various facets of a topic which contributes to the development of their critical thinking and problem solving skills.

Unit studies are typically built around one topic. Some unit studies are based on a period in history, a specific event, or even fictional or historical characters. Other unit studies are built around various scientific discoveries, inventions, or anything else you or your child can imagine.

The best unit studies are those which cover something your child is passionate about.

This integrated approach can include logic, history, reading, literature, writing, photography, social studies, drama, science, math, geography, arts and crafts, learning to draw, art appreciation, music appreciation, physical education and more. This is often referred to as a multi-disciplinary or a thematic approach. It is an experiential, hands-on approach to learning. When children go into such depth, and spend a generous amount of time on each theme, their retention of the subject is higher than when using traditional methods.

> *The best unit studies are those which cover something your child is passionate about.*

For example, when my boys became interested in knights and Medieval England, I developed a unit study for them called ***Time Capsule: Medieval England***[73], which helped them to feel almost as though they were living in Medieval England. They got to wear the clothes, eat the food, forge the weapons, learn about the history, experiment with the scientific inventions of the Middle Ages, listen to the music and more.

---

[73] Time Capsule: Medieval England by Michelle Caskey

Here are 13 benefits of unit studies:

1. Children of all ages and different levels can learn together making this type of learning great for families with varied age ranges.

2. They are lower in cost than traditional curricula – especially if you create your own!

3. The students get an in-depth understanding of each topic – this helps them to develop mastery of the subject and to have longer retention of the material.

4. Since there are no time restraints, the child is given ample time to think, experiment and discover each topic.

5. Students are able to learn using different learning styles because they will study the material using varied activities.

6. Since unit studies are multi-aged, the younger child learns immeasurably from and through the older child. The older child also benefits from teaching what he teaches to the younger child.

7. The creative hands-on projects and activities are great fun.

8. Students learn more detailed information with an in-depth study of a topic.

9. They can hold some children's interest longer than dealing with subjects individually. For example, you may be able to coax a child who doesn't enjoy math to stick with it longer if you present the concepts within the context of a subject he does enjoy.

10. Unit studies encourage the use of imagination, creativity, and thinking skills.

11. Because the topic is presented as a whole, with many memorable experiences, children are less likely to forget what they have learned and experienced!

12. Because the lessons are all interrelated, there are less individual resources to deal with, making lesson planning and teaching simpler.

13. They are a fun way to learn and bring the whole family together!

If you're new to using unit studies, you may want to purchase one where the books and the lesson plans have already been put together for you, like with my ***Time Capsule: Medieval England*** unit study.

If you'd like to try your hand at creating your own unit study, simply do the following:

- Talk with your kids and find a topic that you'd all like to explore in depth.

- Search for good books, both fiction and non-fiction, which can be read during your studies. Be sure to choose books your kids can read as well as some selections you can read aloud to them.

- Search for movies which tie into your subject.

- List the various school subjects you would like to cover with your unit study.

- Search for a variety of activities which your kids can complete that will help them to use as many of their senses as possible, as many learning styles as possible, and will give them as complete a picture of your topic as possible.

- Look for field trips which would help to drive home the lessons you are trying to teach.

Some homeschoolers use unit studies as a break from their regular studies… to try to put some of the fun back into learning. Others use them over summer vacation. And still others use them exclusively.

If you've never tried using a unit study before, you may want to give one a try. Unit studies are a great way to help your kids to enjoy learning again!

Teach Your Boys How to Enjoy Studying History

Why is it that some people absolutely LOVE to study history while others hate it? Is it simply a difference of opinion? Or could it have something to do with the way history is often taught.

If you talk to students who are learning history by reading a textbook, listening to lectures, taking notes, and memorizing dates for a test, you will find that a large percentage of them don't enjoy studying history.

If you talk to students who are learning history by being immersed in the stories, by thinking critically about why things happened the way they did, by actually experiencing the history, you will find that a large percentage of them do enjoy studying history.

History is one of those magical subjects that homeschool moms can help to come alive for their children. All of our children's senses can and should be engaged while learning the history of our world.

Here are 8 ways to teach your boys how to ENJOY studying history:

1. **Allow him to select the time period** – My boys and I have studied quite a few different periods in history. Last year, I planned to focus on American History starting with the American Revolution. We've studied this time period before, however, I wanted to do it again now that my boys were older.

> *All of our children's senses can and should be engaged while learning the history of our world.*

My sons, however, had slightly different thoughts. They wanted to jump ahead and study from World War I to the present. They were more interested in learning about what's currently going on in our world – and they preferred learning about completely newer events versus going back over things they have heard several times. Allowing them to choose the time period helped to ensure that my boys would be more interested in what they were learning.

2. **Break down the timeline over the school year** – After you've decided what time period you will be focusing on, break it down so that you know how long you can spend on each span of years or event.

3. Have him read novels about the time period – Reading historical fiction is a great way for history to come alive for your child. Good historical novels will capture not only what happened, but how people felt about what was happening. These books often recount their triumphs and their struggles. They help our kids to feel as if they have experienced the time period.

4. Have him read nonfiction books about the time period – Reading nonfiction is a great way to be sure that your son is learning the facts of what actually happened. A great guide to find appropriate books is called *All Through the Ages* [74] by Christine Miller.

5. Have him watch movies about the time period – Most boys have at least a somewhat visual learning style. Allowing your son to watch relevant movies is an excellent way for him to enjoy learning about history.

6. Immerse him in the time period – Let him wear the clothes, listen to the music, try the food, forge the weapons... and anything else you can think of that will allow him to experience firsthand what someone from that time period might have experienced. If your son is interested in Medieval England and/or wants to know what it would feel like to be a knight in shining armor or a king, consider trying my *Time Capsule: Medieval England* unit study.

7. Take him on field trips – Any time you can take your son somewhere so that he can see firsthand the way the people lived, you should consider doing it. Visit colonial villages, castles,

---

[74] All Through the Ages by Christine Miller

forts, American Indian villages, Civil War battle sites, etc. Let your son watch reenactments. Even better, help him to participate! A great place to do this is at Colonial Williamsburg.

8. Find some way for him to record what he has learned – Have your son create some sort of project which will help him to remember what he has learned. If he enjoys writing, have him keep a notebook or write a historical novel. If he loves photography, have him create a scrapbook or a photo book. If he's interested in movie making, have him make a movie or a documentary. If he's interested in computers or technology, have him create a webpage or record a podcast. The possibilities are endless!

I remember being in 8th grade and our teacher had us pretend we were part of a wagon train heading west. He helped us plan what supplies we would need to bring and then we were off. Our teacher had set it up so that each table of kids was in a separate wagon – and different things would happen to us depending on the choices that we made.

If we encountered a river, we could cross safely if we had brought enough rope with us. If the journey took longer than we had expected and we ran out of food, we could hunt for meat if we had brought along a gun. Going on the pretend wagon train was one of the biggest adventures I experienced while in school. We all loved it! It was much more exciting to learn in this way than it would have been for us to simply read about wagon trains in a textbook.

We can and should help history come alive for our kids. It takes more effort than simply having them read a textbook... but it's important. As Winston Churchill said,

"Those who do not learn history are doomed to repeat it."

It's worth taking the time for our kids to not only be exposed to the dry facts of history, but for us to help them to love it enough to really want to dig into it!

Should We Stop Teaching Higher Level Math?

You Might Be Surprised!

My boys hate math. When they were younger, they actually liked math. They loved the days of using manipulatives with math – especially if I used something like M&Ms and they got to eat them afterwards!

Even though they don't enjoy math, they're both pretty good at it. When my youngest son was 12 and in 7th grade he was already speeding through Algebra I. But this son still groaned whenever he needed to do his math.

I recently heard a TED talk called, **Why Math Instruction is Unnecessary**[75] by John Bennett which blew my mind. John Bennett, a middle school math teacher, spent almost 12 minutes developing the argument that 99% of the population doesn't need to be taught higher level math. Seriously?!? If there was a way

---

[75] https://www.youtube.com/watch?v=xyowJZxrtbg

to stop having to teach my boys math, I definitely wanted to hear all about it.

John gave the following 4 reasons for why students are taught higher-level math:

1. Math is everywhere – God is a god of order. He has placed mathematical patterns in everything from the spiral of the seeds in a sunflower to the spiral of the galaxies.

2. Math is helpful – It is necessary for most scientific and technological advancement.

3. Math could be required – Our kids might choose a job which will require it someday.

4. Math helps you get good grades – Kids need good grades to get good test scores. They need good test scores to get into a good college. And they need to get into a good college to get a good job.

Some kids are interested in math.

For those kids, John recommends helping them to go as high with math as they would like. He then went on to say that about one half percent of our population becomes an engineer and about one half percent of the population uses some math in their job. The other 99% of the population doesn't need higher mathematics.

John said that forcing ALL kids to learn higher mathematics causes them to feel stupid and stresses them out. And stressed out kids become stressed out adults.

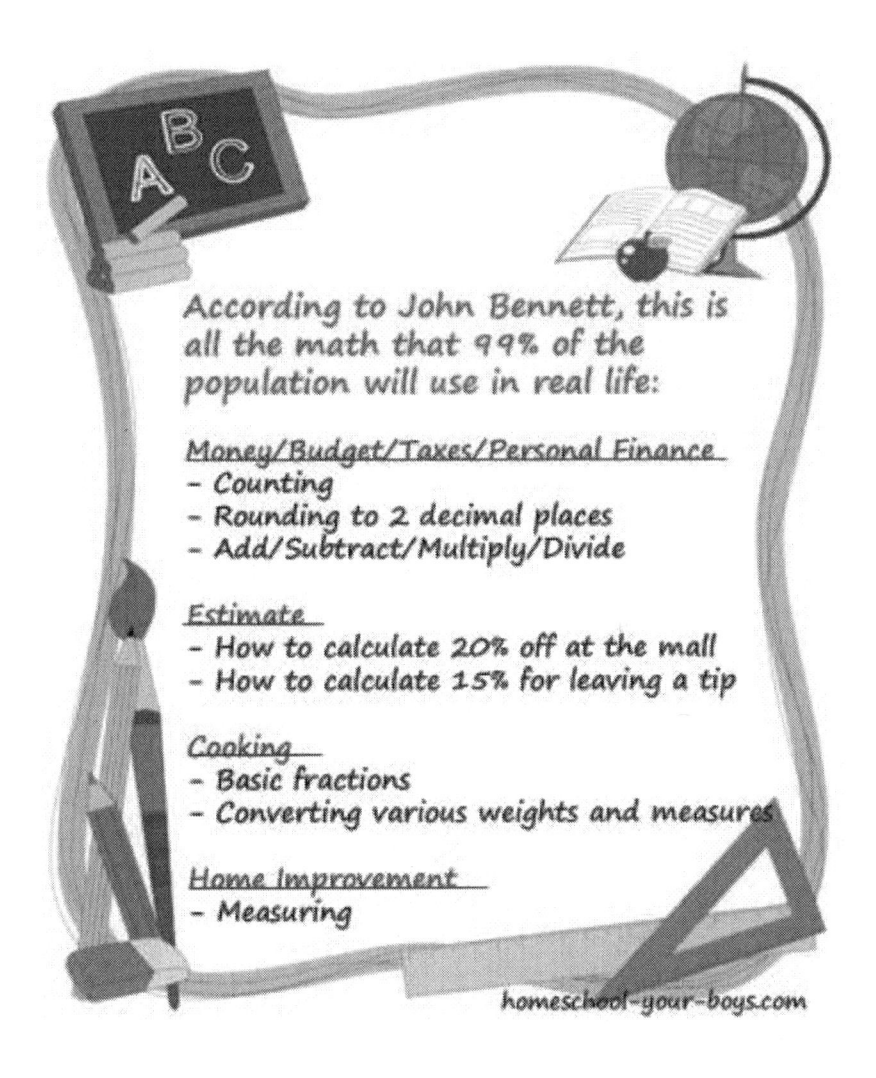

According to John Bennett, this is all the math that 99% of the population will use in real life:

Money/Budget/Taxes/Personal Finance
- Counting
- Rounding to 2 decimal places
- Add/Subtract/Multiply/Divide

Estimate
- How to calculate 20% off at the mall
- How to calculate 15% for leaving a tip

Cooking
- Basic fractions
- Converting various weights and measures

Home Improvement
- Measuring

homeschool-your-boys.com

John emphasized that the majority of this math is learned by age 10. If this is all the math that 99% of the populations needs to know, then why are we requiring all students to take higher level math? John says that it's because we are using math to try to teach kids inductive and deductive reasoning.

Inductive reasoning is when we learn to think in the following manner: If I study for a test, then I will do well on a test. If I do well on a test, then my parents will be happy. So I want to study for my tests to make my parents happy.

Deductive reasoning is when we see a pattern and then come to a conclusion. For example, if we learn to solve an algebraic equation which looks a certain way, then we will learn that every time we see a similar problem, we'll know to solve it that same way.

> *Stressed out kids become stressed out adults.*

John said that quite often, just solving page after page of math problems doesn't help students to make those inductive or deductive leaps. He recommended that it would be more productive to instead let 99% of students work logic puzzles and various games to help them to increase their reasoning skills and problem solving abilities.

Five non-math activities which will help your child to increase their reasoning skills:

- **Video Games** – Believe it or not, video games actually help kids learn to make quick and accurate decisions. They help them develop better hand-eye coordination as well as enhancing their spatial intelligence. There are many games kids enjoy playing which aren't filled with violence or crime.

Minecraft is a game my boys LOVE to play. They also love playing fast action sports games on the Wii U such as NBA 2K13 and Madden NFL 13. And they love the Lego series of games such as The Hobbit and The Lego Movie.

- **Board Games** – Board games are excellent at helping kids to become more number smart, word smart, and people smart. All games force the players to make decisions, come up with good strategies, and interact with the other players.

- **Sports and Exercise** – Being physically active boosts blood flow to all parts of the body including the brain. Complex reasoning, concentration, and thinking speed are all enhanced when the brain is supplied with freshly oxygenated blood. The more your kids move the better they will be able to think. Physical activity also has the positive benefits of increasing creativity, promoting clear thinking, improving coordination, and decreasing depression.

- **Music Training** – Research shows that the brains of kids who learn to play a musical instrument work differently than the brains of kids who don't receive any musical training. *"When you're a musician and you're playing an instrument, you have to be using more of your brain,"* says Dr. Eric Rasmussen, chair of the Early Childhood Music Department at the Peabody Preparatory of The Johns Hopkins University. Musical training boosts a child's IQ, increases their spatial intelligence, and develops their skill to solve multistep problems such as the ones encountered in architecture, engineering, math, and computer science.

- **Critical Thinking** – Teaching our kids critical thinking is an excellent way to increase their reasoning skills. Have them solve logic puzzles. Encourage them to ask questions. Help them to consider alternate explanations and solutions to problems. Help them to notice logical fallacies in thinking. Encourage them to reason about ethical, moral, and public policy issues. Teach them debating skills.

Should we stop teaching our kids higher level math? I can't answer that question for you and your family. I can only say that my husband and I will be praying about this matter and see which way we feel God is leading us.

One big thing to consider is that higher math skills are necessary if you're planning to have your child take the ACT or SAT. There are ways around these tests, however, if you want to send your kids to college but don't want to have them take these tests. (I wrote more about this in the following chapter.)

We are planning to at least give a lower emphasis to math and a higher emphasis to critical thinking skills. Long term, however, we haven't made a final decision about how to proceed. My boys ENJOY learning about logic and completing logic puzzles – they cringe when they have to complete math problems… We'll definitely be doing some more pondering and praying! I hope that you will, too.

Bachelor's Degree by Age 18

How did Thomas Jefferson graduate from the college of William and Mary after completing all of his studies in two years... and at the age of 18? Why is the average age at which students graduate from college rising dramatically? Is it possible today to help your child graduate with his bachelor's degree by age 18?

When I had a chance to attend a seminar entitled *A Bachelor's Degree by Age 18?* I was skeptical but decided to hear what the presenter had to say. This seminar, taught by Woody Robertson of College Plus, was filled with information I had never before heard. Woody talked about the trend for students to graduate later and later in life, the reason schools became grade segregated, and how it's possible for your child to enroll in high school and college at the same time.

Students Graduating Later and Later

In America, educating methods have changed drastically over time. In the 1600s through the early 1800s, the regular method of educating children was either the homeschool or mentor model of education. Affluent families would hire a teacher to live with their family and educate their children. Parents of less means would educate their children themselves.

This was the standard way of educating children for the first couple of hundred years that people lived on this continent. We have many great thinkers who emerged during this time including our founding fathers. No one would ever think to accuse these men of having received a substandard education.

For much of the 1800s, children were educated in one room schoolhouses. This change came about because many people were moving out to the frontier and there were book shortages out west. Parents decided to bind together to educate their children, allowing them to hire one teacher to teach several children. This enabled students to share what few books they could gather.

This method was also very successful. As most education experts would agree, it is extremely helpful for older students to help teach younger students. This allows them to cement the knowledge in their own minds as they relay the information to other students.

How and Why Grade Segregation Came About

The early 1900s to the present has seen the birth of the grade segregated classroom in our country. This initially came about for a number of reasons. First, World War I was looming and America saw Germany as a threat. Teachers wanted to be sure they didn't skip any information while teaching their students to try to ensure that our children would come out more highly educated than would the German students.

Another factor which was less benevolent was introduced by several financiers. Before this time, students would graduate from grammar school and would go directly to college. The idea of sending students to high school before college was introduced by men such as Carnegie, Morgan, Ford and Rockefeller. Requiring four years of high school meant that many new facilities would need to be built to house the students who were being educated for an additional four years.

A third factor which contributed to starting grade segregation was that the industrial revolution was beginning around this time. Some of those same financiers needed schools to produce thousands of workers for their factories. These men surmised that if the length of education were increased by an additional four years, many students might become tired of learning and would decline the option of going on to college. They wanted workers who had "just enough" education to be content working on the assembly lines.

There is a lot more information available concerning the current model of education and how it all came about. I would suggest you read one of these books to get even more background, if you are interested:

- *Dumbing Us Down*[76] by John Taylor Gatto
- *A Thomas Jefferson Education*[77] by Oliver DeMille

---

[76] Dumbing Us Down by John Taylor Gatto
[77] A Thomas Jefferson Education by Oliver DeMille

- ***An Underground History of American Education***[78] by John Taylor Gatto (FREE PDF available on internet)

Dual Credit/Enrollment Options

So… how do we help our kids to complete high school and college within four years? We basically have them complete both at the same time. There are three different ways to make this happen:

- **Community College Option** – You can have your child enroll in a community college and have him complete classes which will count toward his high school and his college education at the same time. This has the advantage of being inexpensive; however, Woody pointed out that the average community college student is pretty unmotivated and isn't necessarily the type of person with which you would want your child to be spending their day.

- **Online Courses** – This is a way to help your student get a traditional education. The problem with this method is that it can be expensive and you don't have any control over the content of what they are learning.

- **Credit by Exam** – This is the method that Woody recommended in his seminar. This method allows you to teach your student as you normally would and then have him take a test which will give him college credit in the future. There are three different types of tests that can be taken:

---

[78] An Underground History of American Education by John Taylor Gatto

DSST Exams, AP Exams, and CLEP exams. CLEP tests are what Woody recommended in the seminar.

According to Woody, there are five different General Ed CLEPS that everyone should take:

- College Composition
- Humanities
- Social Science and History
- Natural Sciences
- College Mathematics
- Nuts and Bolts of Dual Enrollment

How do you know what high school requirements to record on their transcript when your student is using the credit by exam method? Basically, if he taked a three credit exam, that is worth 1/2 of a high school credit. If he takes a six credit exam, that is worth one full high school credit.

What about declaring a college major?

What if your student doesn't have a clear idea of what he wants to do when he graduates? Woody suggests keeping their undergraduate degree as broad as possible. Have your child get a BA in either Communications or Business and then he can get more specialized if he decides to do some graduate work.

Woody also suggests pursuing internships to help your student try to test different areas of their interest. He suggests basing your major on your student's interests and passions versus identifying a specific job they think they might want to have.

Modular Approach to Study

If you decide to go this route with your student, you may want to use a modular approach to study, focusing on one subject at a time and studying similar subjects in succession. You can read more about the benefits of this approach in these books by John Taylor Gatto:

- *A Different Kind of Teacher*[79]
- *Weapons of Mass Instruction*[80]
- *The Exhausted School: Bending the Bars of Traditional Education*[81]

A suggested daily schedule would be the following:

- Study English and Math for the first two hours of each day.

- Spend the next 4-5 hours studying one specific subject. This is the subject you are studying with the goal of taking an exam for which to earn college credit.

- After your student finishes studying for their specific subject, have him take a practice test. Have him take it immediately after finishing the subject. When he does well on the practice test, have him take the actual test. You will want to have your student start taking these tests by his junior year at the latest.

One other practical item you should consider is whether the college your child wants to attend accepts CLEP or other exam

---

[79] A Different Kind of Teacher by John Taylor Gatto
[80] Weapons of Mass Instruction by John Taylor Gatto
[81] The Exhausted School by John Taylor Gatto

credits. If the school your student wants to attend only accepts 10 hours of credits, it doesn't do any good to have him take 20 hours worth of exams.

The other positive aspect of your student having CLEP credits is that this proves that they are able to handle college-level classes and they will no longer be required to take either the ACT or the SAT. They will be considered a transfer student instead of an incoming freshman.

Unfortunately, there are many more scholarships available to freshman than to transfer students. Because of this, I've had some homeschool parents recommend that your child still take the ACT or SAT and apply to colleges as a freshman. After begin accepted, they then tell the college about their CLEP credits. You'll have to decide which way will work best for your child depending on how well they do taking tests.
By the way, two fully accredited schools which accept lots of CLEP hours are Thomas Edison State College and Excelsior State College.

There is a ton of information here and I hope that by reading this, you'll realize that it is possible for your child to complete at least some of their high school and college classes at the same time. If you're intrigued and would like to find out more, there is an organization called College Plus[82] that would love to help you get started. There are also plenty of books out there to help you through this process on your own.

---

[82] https://collegeplus.org/

Character Education Through Volunteering

Character education is something that most homeschool parents will admit is important – but sometimes it can be hard to figure out how to add anything else to your already massive stack of teacher's manuals.

Character building doesn't have to be another subject that you tack onto the end of your day. In fact, I would argue that helping your children to develop positive character traits is actually more effective if you use hands-on, real world methods.

One way you can do this is by volunteering with your children.

Volunteering has made a big difference in our lives. Summertime is a great time to add volunteer time to your day, since most of us have a somewhat modified schedule during the summer months and aren't quite as busy with our regular subjects.

There are many positive reasons to volunteer:

- **It's great for your kids** – Nothing builds character in your children more helping others selflessly.

- **It's great for others** – There are so many organizations that depend on volunteer help. The average family has become so busy with two incomes and all of their various activities that they don't have time in their day for volunteering. There are many places that need us!

- **It's great for your child's transcript/resume** – Keep track of the various places at which your child volunteers and you can use this information on college applications, scholarship applications, etc. Not only does it help other people it also helps your child.

No matter how young your children are, they can help to pick up litter in state and county parks. There are also many organizations that need help stuffing envelopes, with general maintenance such as cleaning, etc.

> *Helping your children develop positive character traits is more effective if you use hands-on, real world methods.*

Some fun volunteer opportunities we have discovered are working at animal shelters and sanctuaries. We worked at a dog sanctuary in our area one summer and our tasks included such things as walking dogs, playing with dogs, and teaching them tricks. What boy wouldn't want to spend one afternoon a week doing those kinds of activities?!?

Another rewarding experience was when our homeschool co-op put on a musical for a local nursing home. It was such a blessing to see the faces of the residents as the children performed. They were thrilled! Afterward, the kids mingled with the residents and gave them homemade cards. My sons got into some interesting conversations with a few of the residents. I think that experience will stay with them for a long time.

One of my friends and her sons go to a local school and help pack lunches for some of the less fortunate kids in their district so that they'll have something to eat when they get home at night and on weekends.

Another friend and her son volunteer at the local library by shelving books and doing other odd jobs.

Finding Volunteer Opportunities

If you are interested in volunteering somewhere and aren't sure where to go, you can always check with the United Way[83] in your area. They keep lists of different organizations who have contacted them requesting help. You can also check Google to see if anything comes up on the internet.

If you are unable to find any suitable opportunities in these ways, don't be afraid to call organizations directly and offer your assistance. Homeless shelters, food banks, women's shelters, or any other non-profit organization would be great places to call.

You can also call virtually any organization which counts on federal or state funding and offer to help. Most of these places have experienced cuts in their funding and have had to let go of staff – they would be thrilled to have someone come in and help them on a regular basis.

---

[83] http://www.volunteermatch.org/

Try volunteering at a variety of places. This is almost like working a free internship and gives your children some job experience. It also helps them to determine their likes and dislikes so that they'll have a better idea of what they want to pursue for a career someday.

The next time you think about purchasing a character education curriculum for your children, try volunteering with them instead. Getting this real world, hands-on experience is not only good for others… it's also good for your kids!

The Benefits of Being a Student Entrepreneur

When my boys hit their tween years, we started allowing them to earn a small allowance for doing extra chores around the house and yard. They have enjoyed being able to save up their money to buy different items, such as Legos, that they otherwise wouldn't receive until their birthday or Christmas. They quickly realized that it takes a long time to be able to buy anything with their allowance money alone.

One year, my younger son decided he'd like to create some sort of business in order to earn money faster. Because we have a large backyard, my husband and I steered him toward being a student entrepreneur by growing and selling pumpkins. It didn't take long for our older son to also jump on the band wagon.

The boys purchased their seeds with allowance money. They bought $3.25 worth of seeds. We all pitched in clearing more ground next to our family garden so they would have somewhere to grow the pumpkins. My husband spent many hours busting sod and putting up fencing to help the boys with their business.

The boys also spent many hours helping to bust sod and using the wheelbarrow to haul the sod from the garden to the woods next to our house. We showed the boys how to plant their pumpkin seeds... which was the easiest part of the job.

All summer long, the boys faithfully carried water out to the garden to water their pumpkins. We had an extremely hot and dry summer, so they had to water just about every day. They were thrilled to watch the vines grow, to see the flowers bloom, and to view the pumpkins as they grew bigger and bigger.

When the boys sold their pumpkins that fall they earned $99. Not bad for a $3.25 investment and some sweat equity! They had more potential customers than they did pumpkins; so, the next year they broke MORE sod and planted even MORE pumpkins.

My boys learned so many lessons from being student entrepreneurs:

1. Perseverance – For awhile, it didn't look like they were going to get any pumpkins at all. They had to replant a few seeds and push a few more back into the ground. The first several weeks of their new business was a bit discouraging for them. After a few weeks of continuing to water, however, the first vines appeared and the boys were glad they hadn't given up.

2. Hard Work Pays Off – My boys didn't feel like watering every day. They didn't enjoy having to haul bunches and bunches of sod from the garden to the woods. The task of weeding wasn't enjoyable to them. Once the pumpkins were sold and the money was in hand, however, they were so glad that they had spent all of that time in the garden!

3. Don't Waste Your Money – My boys have always had a habit of spending every penny of birthday, Christmas, and allowance money on toys. No matter how much we tried to persuade them to save it so that they could buy something of more value, they would resist us. After working so hard to earn their pumpkin money, however, they came up with the idea of saving their money to purchase their own laptop. They are starting to understand the value of money.

4. Computer Skills – My boys took their business seriously. They learned how to use a spreadsheet to track the hours they spent working in the garden. They also recorded the money that was spent on their business.

5. Teamwork – When there is a job to be done, my boys haven't always been the best at doing what needs to be done. They both tend to try not to do any more than 50% of the work so that they won't feel like they are being taken advantage of by their brother.

During their pumpkin business, they learned to appreciate the division of labor. One of my boys was better at handling the wheelbarrow – so one took care of that responsibility. The other struggled with the wheelbarrow so he ended up being the one to hurl the sod into the wheelbarrow. Instead of fighting about who was working the hardest they ended up appreciating the fact that they were both handling separate tasks. They learned to delegate as well. Especially my oldest son!

6. Responsibility – Every day the boys had the responsibility of watering their pumpkins. They were also responsible for keeping their patch weeded. We tried not to remind them and to let them remember these duties on their own. As the summer went on, they got better and better at remembering. They found that it was easier to keep up on the weeding than to let it go and have to have the terrible job of clearing out an overgrown weed patch!

7. Goal Setting – The boys spent a considerable amount of time trying to decide how much money they'd like to try to earn the next year. They used the information they recorded in their spreadsheets to project how much additional land they would need to clear and how many pumpkins they would need to plant in order to achieve their goals.

8. Selling Skills – The boys sold their own pumpkins. They told everyone they knew that they were growing pumpkins during the summer. Once the pumpkins were ready, they made some phone calls to people who had previously expressed an interest in purchasing some. It definitely pushed them out of their comfort zone to make these phone calls – but people were very receptive and patient with them.

9. Good Customer Service – While delivering pumpkins to customers, they were extremely polite. They offered to help carry the pumpkins to their cars. They thanked everyone.

10. Integrity – While accepting payments, one customer misunderstood the prices and paid them $2 less than what they actually owed. My boys didn't count the money until after the customer had left – so that was one lesson. The next customer, however, accidentally gave them an extra dollar. They hurriedly counted the money as she was walking away. As soon as they realized what she had done, one son ran after her to give her dollar back. She smiled and told them they could keep it. But it took great integrity for them to be honest, especially when they had just been shorted by a previous customer.

Being student entrepreneurs has been an amazing learning experience for my sons. They have gained more responsibility and maturity from this experience than I ever dreamed was possible in the span of a few months time.

If your son is interested in starting his own business, I would highly recommend it. The type of business he runs will depend on his age and ability – but kids can learn so much from running a business whether it is something simple such as a lemonade stand or a lawn mowing businesses, or if it is more complicated such as an internet business or self-publishing their own book.

Encourage your children to try being student entrepreneurs. You'll be amazed at all the new skills they'll learn!

Outdoor Learning Activities

Do you give your boys outside fun? Where are they spending the bulk of their day?

Are you giving your boys outside fun throughout their school day? Or do they spend most of their time sitting inside with their noses in books, staring at the TV and watching a computer screen?

Remember being a kid and riding your bike all day long? Or building forts out in the woods? Or picking berries and being gone for hours until we finally had to go home for food or we thought we'd starve!?!

Today's generation of children is growing up differently than we did. According to the CDC, children are six times more likely to play a video game on a typical day than to ride a bike. This type of behavior is having an impact on their bodies and on their brains.

One of the great things about homeschooling boys is that we have complete freedom in how we spend our time throughout the day. And not just during the summer, either.

There are several great ways to give our boys outside fun and active learning throughout the school year:

1. Biking Trips - Biking is a wonderful activity to incorporate into your homeschool gym class. As a child, I remember playing dodge ball, climbing ropes, and doing lots of other activities in gym class which I couldn't easily do at home. Either they required specialized equipment, like parachutes or expensive sports gear – or they required a lot of kids!

I feel strongly that a good homeschool gym class should train our sons to enjoy activities which they can continue to do for a lifetime – and bike riding is a wonderful example of this kind of activity. Riding bikes helps your sons to stay healthy and it's a great way to give your boys outside fun, as well.

There are many wonderful lessons which you can integrate into a family bike trip:

- **Art** – Have your son draw pictures of wildlife, flowers, and other interesting sights that you encounter.

- **Character Building** – Teach your sons to be courteous to cars and other bikers on your journey. Your family can also participate in many different biking fund raisers to help the less fortunate.

- **Deductive Reasoning** – Try out geocaching or letter boxing while on a bike ride. You can find out more about these activities by doing a Google search.

- **Geography** – Be sure to teach your sons about the area they are travelling through. You can also put up a large map on the wall and track your various trips on the map. If you often bike the same routes, take a virtual trip. Pick a faraway destination, log the number of miles you bike, and draw lines between your city and your "destination" city. Teach lessons about the geography you're "passing through," so that your sons become familiar with the world around them.

- **History** – Explore different historic locations throughout your trip – your sons can also research the history of the specific bike trail you plan to take.

- **Mapping Skills** – Let your son be the navigator both beforehand, while determining your route, as well as during the trip.

- **Math** – Let your son estimate how much time the ride will take, as well as calculate the mileage and the finances for the trip.

- **Photography** – Let your son take photos along the way.

- **Science** – Document wildlife that you encounter along the way. Some adventurous sons will even want to collect road kill that they can dissect later.

- **Writing** – Have your son write in his journal about the experience.

Take a family bike trip and your sons will enjoy their homeschool gym class – and they will also start down the path to a lifetime of physical fitness.

2. Field Trips for Homeschool – Going on field trips are some of the most thrilling real life lessons that we can give to our children. Taking a field trip is an awesome way to give boys outside fun.

I will never forget the excitement, when I was a child, of watching a bunch of Kellogg's Corn Flakes moving down a conveyor belt and then getting to taste a box of fresh cereal at the end of the tour. Or going to the fire station and getting to spray their big hose. Field trips taken with your children will stay with them for many years to come.

If we want children to engage in meaningful learning experiences that connect with their real lives, we need to make education relevant for them. Schools are somewhat limited in how much they can get children outside of the classroom.

Homeschool parents have much more freedom in this area. Since book work only consumes 2-4 hours per day, depending on your curriculum, we have a lot of time left over to get our boys outside.

Fieldtrips for homeschool are a fun way to incorporate real world learning into their day.

There are so many places to visit:

- Museums
- Zoos
- Nature centers
- Local Factories and Businesses
- Doctor's Offices and Fire Stations, etc.
- Historic Locations
- Farms

Talk to everyone you know to see who would be willing to allow you to come visit their place of business – or allow your son to job shadow him for a day. The more you allow your boys to experience a variety of job situations, the more accurately they will be able to determine what type of career they might like to pursue as they get older.

3. Gardening for Kids - If you've never actually planted a garden with your children, this year is the perfect time to start. Gardening is one of the best learning opportunities that you can give to your child. Obviously, your child will learn scientific principles of horticulture as he plants a seed and watches it grow.

But there are so many other things that you child will learn while gardening:

- He will learn perseverance as he goes out to the garden day after day to pull weeds and water the plants.

- He will learn patience as he waits for the plants to grow – and then waits for harvest time when he can finally taste the fruits (and vegetables) of his labor.

- He will learn planning and math skills as he helps you to come up with a plan for your garden – including properly spacing the plants according to their differing needs.

- He will learn where food comes from and all of the different processes it takes to go from the seed packet to the table.

- He will learn ingenuity as he comes up with different ways to prevent pests from getting into the garden and ruining the crops.

- He will learn how to appreciate good, honest hard work

And the list goes on and on. Even if you don't have a big yard, you can still find room to garden. Try making a container garden on your balcony or deck. Investigate community gardens in your area. Ask about planting a garden on your rooftop deck. Where there's a will there's a way!

Plant a garden with your child. It's too amazing of a learning experience for you to let it pass your family by.

4. Hiking and Nature Walks – If you find that you have a hard time keeping your children interested in their studies once the weather turns warmer, take your boys hiking. A few hours of outdoor education is a great way to exercise their bodies while learning an amazing amount of things about the world in which we live.

Things for boys to learn about while on a hike:

- **Animal tracks** – identify which animals make which tracks

- **Botany** – identify flowers, trees, grass

- **Geology** – identify different rocks, minerals, soil

- **Insects** – identify which ones would be edible in an emergency situation?

- **Biology** – identify mammals, reptiles, birds, etc.

Before you go, you may want to consult a trail map for the area you're planning to take your boys hiking. Hiking trails vary in length as well as difficulty level. You don't want to end up halfway down a difficult trail, miles from your car, without enough energy to get you back safely. Look for trail maps in field guides, on-line, or at the visitor's center of the park you'll be hiking.

Things to think about bringing with you or wearing on a hike – depending on the season:

- Water bottle or canteen
- Healthy snacks like nuts or granola bars
- Sunscreen
- Insect repellent
- Rain jacket
- Hat to keep off the sun
- Tennis shoes or hiking boots
- Long pants and long sleeves (to avoid poison ivy if you will be wandering into the woods)
- Warm layers of clothes, warm hat, mittens
- Nature journals or cameras

Be sure to hike in a variety of terrain, so that your boys will become familiar with different types of habitats:

- Coastal and beach areas
- Inside abandoned mines or caves
- Prairie
- Forest or Jungle
- Wetlands
- Mountainous Areas

If your boys are already avid hikers, you can spice up any journey by turning it into a scavenger hunt. Make up lists of things that you can see, hear, touch, smell… and (for the very adventurous) taste. You can even award prizes at the end of the trip for the person who found the most items, the biggest item, the dirtiest item, etc. Boys love variety, so the more twists you add to the hunt the more they will enjoy it.

Taking your boys hiking and giving them some outside fun is a great way to keep them interested in learning over the long haul.

5. Homeschool Camping Ideas - Do you need some great homeschool camping ideas? Are you planning a camping trip and have no idea what to do with your sons while you're out in the great outdoors?

Camping is one of the best ways to teach your sons without them even realizing it. Homeschooling your sons while out in nature is lots of fun – but you'll want to be prepared with lots of camping ideas before you go. The most natural way to learn is to teach from situations as they present themselves and not to try to force specific events to happen.

While camping, it will be obvious to you that you aren't in control of the weather or your environment. If you are prepared with many possible homeschooling ideas beforehand, you'll be ready to teach your sons regardless of the circumstances you might encounter.

Here are some great camping ideas that you can try with your boys on your next family trip:

- **Animal Tracks** – Finding animal tracks can be so much fun. Identifying them is even more gratifying. Depending on your own skills, you can attempt to follow them and see how far you can track the animals. Be careful which animals you attempt to locate. Obviously, raccoon and deer would be safer to track than coyotes or bears!

- **Bird Watching** – You can identify birds by sight – or sit quietly and try to identify them by sound.

- **Campfires** – Roasting marshmallows and hot dogs is a favorite past time for our sons. Also, take this opportunity to instruct your sons in the proper art of campfire building. They'll love it!

- **Field Guides** – You can get amazing field guides on everything from mammals to birds to flowers to frogs – and you can get guides that are specific to your area! We have found the guides by Stan Tekiela[84] to be helpful. Get the guides with the audio CDs if you can. You will be amazed at how quickly your boys will learn the sounds of the frogs and

---

[84] Field guides by Stan Tekiela

the birds. And they're great to listen to in the car on long rides.

- **Fishing** – What little boy wouldn't want to learn to fish? Whether you cook your catch or throw it back, he will learn a lot from this experience. And let him hunt for his own bait as well.

- **Hiking** – When you choose your camping location, be sure to pick one which has hiking trails. Most state parks and national parks have many trails. Pick up trail maps at the office so that you can explore them all.

- **Maps** – Speaking of maps, let your sons be the navigators when you are hiking. Bring along a compass and let them learn how to use that as well.

- **Mushroom Hunting** – Depending on where and when you camp, you may be able to hunt for mushrooms. If you decide to give this a try, make sure you know what you are gathering before you eat them!

- **Nature Journals** – At the end of every day, have your sons write about their experiences and draw pictures in a sketchbook as well. If they are interested in photography, they can leave room for any pictures they may have taken throughout the day as well.

- **Scavenger Hunts** – Boys love scavenger hunts. They help them to practice their reading skills as well as their deductive reasoning. Write your clues so that they will help them to practice many of the other skills they've learned while camping as well.

- **Sports** – Bring along Frisbees, baseball gloves and balls, footballs, and other sports equipment that your sons enjoy. Downtime at the camp site can be a wonderful time to practice these skills as well.

- **Stars** – Bring along a star map for your area and for the proper season. The more remote your location, the more easily you will be able to see the stars.

- **Survival Skills** - Boys love to learn survival skills and camping is a great time to try these out. Some of the more useful skills would be:

    o Making a fire without matches – Try a flint and knife, first, and once they have that mastered let them try it with two sticks. There are several methods for making fire this way. This will be an adventure for the whole family!
    o Looking for edible plants and bugs
    o Tying knots
    o Signaling for help
    o Purifying water
    o Building shelters
    o Drying out wet wood and grass

- **Swimming** – If your boys haven't taken formal swimming lessons, this is a great time to teach them. At the very least, teach them how to tread water and how to float on their backs. That way, if they ever find themselves in water over their head, they can hold their own until they are able to be pulled out of the water.

- **Tents** – If you and your sons are going to get the most learning out of a camping experience, you need to use a tent. Leave the RVs and trailers at home. Also, leave behind the TVs, hand-held video games, and anything else that might distract your sons from nature. Yes, this type of vacation is less relaxing for the parents; but, you need to remember what your reason was for getting your sons outside in the first place!

- **Weather Wisdom** – Identify the clouds and what types of weather they usually precede.

Nature is the best classroom for your sons – and homeschooling is something you can do with your children whether at home or on vacation. I hope you try several of these homeschool camping ideas with your family – to give your boys outside fun. When you make lessons relevant and enjoyable for your sons, you will be amazed at how eager they will be to learn.

6. Physical Education at home - When developing a homeschool gym class for our children, we need to keep in mind that many of our kids today seem to work hard to avoid physical activity. They prefer playing video games and watching TV to running, jumping, and active playing.

Most kids would also rather eat junk food than anything nutritious. This explains why 13% of 7-12 year olds have at least 1 risk factor for heart disease. How can you make sure that your sons aren't part of that 13%? Make sure they get at least 20-30 minutes of aerobic exercise 3-4 times a week.

When I was a child, I attended public school and gym class was something I dreaded. I was terrified of being the last kid picked for the dodge ball team, I couldn't hit a softball very far, and I would rather be reading than running. My best friend and I made a point of getting out of gym as often as possible. The emphasis in our gym class was on performance rather than on learning physical skills which could be continued for a lifetime. And was it really necessary to require communal showers in middle school?!?! Talk about embarrassing!

We all know it is important for children to grow up learning how to eat properly and exercise – and we want to make sure our sons benefit from this type of training.

Many parents focus on team sports with their children and these are great. We should also try to also work in some individual activities such as swimming, running, biking or hiking because these are things our kids can continue to participate in well into adulthood.

And whether or not a child is skilled in sports, it is still important that they engage in physical activity of some type. When given a broad enough range of choices, all kids will find activities that they enjoy.

Nothing can replace some unstructured time spent outside digging in the dirt, exploring a creek, riding a bike, etc. Boys love to explore and this is an activity that should definitely be encouraged. With a little bit of thought, you can enhance your son's education by giving your boys outside fun and incorporating active learning into his day.

How to Start Homeschooling

I hear from people all the time asking me how they can pull their children out of school and start homeschooling. Unfortunately, I'm not surprised by this question. School classrooms are typically set up to provide optimal learning conditions for girls not boys. Most boys need to be more active than the typical schoolroom allows.

If you're asking yourself, "How do I start homeschooling?" you are in the right place. Here are some helpful tips to get you headed in the right direction:

Step One – The first thing you need to do is to find out about the homeschooling laws where you live. If you live in America, you can do this by going to the Homeschool Legal Defense Association's[85] website. Hopefully the state you live in is a low regulation state so that you won't have as many hoops to go through to keep your children home from public school. The less regulations your state has, the more easily you can start homeschooling them.

---

[85] http://www.hslda.org/hs/default.asp

If you live outside of America, you should still be able to Google the name of your country and the search terms "homeschooling laws" to determine how you can legally homeschool your children.

Where I live, if you start homeschooling your child from the beginning, you don't even have to notify your school district of your intent. If you are pulling your child out of public school, then the notification requirements are still minimal. So don't feel that this step needs to be difficult. Fulfill the requirements for where you live and move on to step two.

Step Two – Next, you will need to choose a curriculum. We are so fortunate these days that there are a plethora of curriculum options out there for homeschoolers. There are so many different products with different strengths and amounts of hands-on learning from which to choose. The important thing to remember is that just because you decided to try a publisher this year, that doesn't mean you need to continue using it throughout your entire homeschooling experience.

Every year you will want to take a step back and evaluate the curriculum you've been using. Ask yourself how it has been working for you and your children? Were there enough hands-on activities to keep the enjoyment in your boys' learning?

There are great guides available which will help you to make a well-informed decision before you make a purchase you might later regret.

Step Three – Once your materials arrive, you need to get organized. Look over the entire year of curriculum to determine what materials you will need to acquire that you wouldn't normally have around the house. Then, every week, take a look at the next week's curriculum to get the schoolwork organized and ready for your child to perform.

This sounds harder than it is. Simply familiarize yourself with the teacher's manuals, gather the necessary materials, and you're all set. I always put each day's assignments into separate folders to make daily preparation quick and simple. That way I can get each day ready on the weekend and just switch folders each morning before we begin.

> *This sounds harder than it is.*

Step Four – Set up an area where you will store your materials and where your children will complete their schoolwork. You do NOT need a separate classroom available in order to homeschool. My sons do their schoolwork at the dining room table, on the living room floor, standing in the kitchen, wandering around outside, and while sitting on the couch.

You may want to get your child a clipboard so that they can take their assignments wherever they feel most comfortable. When the weather is nice it is fun to do assignments at a picnic table outside or to let them going into a tree fort to complete their reading. Think outside of the box!

Step Five – Get started. You may want to check out a homeschooling support group in your area. There are also many organizations which provide field trips, sports, and many other learning opportunities for homeschooled children.

With these tips in mind, you should be able to start homeschooling your children with minimal stress. Have fun and enjoy this wonderful time that you will be able to spend with your children. Remember, your lack of formal training as a teacher will be more than made up for by your love for your kids and your desire to see them excel to their full and unique potential.

Are you Letting God Write Your Homeschool Story?

During the summer, I do a lot of planning our coming homeschool year. Now that I have a son who is high school age, I've been writing course descriptions, creating reading lists, and updating transcripts.

I try very hard to come up with classes which will satisfy college admissions boards should my boys choose to attend someday... but will also have a twist which will make them interesting and relevant to my sons.

Like most homeschool moms, I spend a lot of time during the summer planning out our coming homeschool year.

A few days ago, I was pondering next year while making lunch. I turned on the radio and the song **"Write Your Story"** by Francesca Battistelli came on. I've often found myself humming along with songs on the radio... sort of mindlessly. This time, however, the words jumped out at me from the airwaves and made me feel quite convicted.

Here are the words if you are unfamiliar with this particular song:

They say
You're the King of everything
The One who taught the wind to sing
The Source of the rhythm my heart keeps beating
They say
You can give the blind their sight
And You can bring the dead to life
You can be the hope my soul's been seekin'

I wanna tell You now that I believe it
I wanna tell You now that I believe it
I do, that You can make me new, oh

CHORUS
I'm an empty page
I'm an open book
Write Your story on my heart
Come on and make Your mark
Author of my hope
Maker of the stars
Let me be Your work of art
Won't You write Your story on my heart

Write Your story, write Your story
Come on and write Your story, write Your story
Won't You write Your story on my heart

My Life
I know it's never really been mine
So do with it whatever You like
I don't know what Your plan is
But I know it's good, yeah

I wanna tell You now that I believe in
I wanna tell You now that I believe in
In You, so do what You do, oh

CHORUS

Write Your story, write Your story
Come on and write Your story, write Your story
Won't You write Your story on my heart

I want my history
To be Your legacy
Go ahead and show this world
What You've done in me
And when the music fades
I want my life to say

I let You write your story, write Your story
Write Your story, write Your story

CHORUS

Write Your story, write Your story
Come on and write Your story, write Your story
Won't You write Your story on my heart

Several lines from this song stuck out to me:

- I'm an empty page. I'm an open book. Write Your story on my heart. Come on and make Your mark.
- My Life – I know it's never really been mine so do with it whatever You like.
- I don't know what Your plan is but I know it's good.

Those words really hit me. Am I am empty page? Am I willing to have God write His story on my heart? Am I open to whatever He wants to do with my life? With my sons' lives? With my homeschool plans?

Ouch! I'm afraid that too often I run ahead and come up with a plan and then ask God afterwards if He will bless whatever I've come up with. Does that found familiar to you?

The safest place for myself and my boys to be is smack dab in the middle of God's plan. I want to be where God wants me to be. I want my boys to do what God wants them to do.

When is the last time I asked God any of the following questions:

- What He wants them to study?
- Which extracurricular activities He thinks would be beneficial for them?
- Whether He would like me to say "yes" or "no" when asked to volunteer for something at church?

Do I ask Him these questions? Or do I assume that I know what's best and plow forward without praying about it?

So I ask you: Who plans your homeschool schedule? You? A school board? A future college admissions office? Or God?

Are you letting God write your homeschool story? I hope that you will consider who's in charge of your homeschool while you're coming up with plans for next year. I know I will!

Are We Focused on the Right Things?

One night, I was sitting at the picnic table in our backyard waiting for our dog to do his business. It had been a long day and I was exhausted. As I sat there, I felt my shoulders sagging and my head drooping down.

After sitting that way for several minutes, a bird flew overhead and got my attention. As I turned around I gasped. There was a beautiful sunset taking place behind me. A flock of geese was flying into the bright orange sky and it was all taking place in front of the lovely barn and alfalfa field next door. I had been so focused on waiting out the mundane matter before me that I had almost missed the stunning scene which was taking place all around me.

As I watched the beautiful scene, I couldn't help but compare it to our homeschool experience. Could it be that sometimes I'm so focused on choosing the right curriculum, creating lesson plans, and crafting other details of our day that I fail to sit back and enjoy the splendor of the experience?

Are We Focused on the Right Things?

I think we do this all too often. As homeschool moms, we are surrounded by our children on a daily basis. Sometimes the chaos of the never-ending demands, the quarreling, the whining, and the unceasing questions can cause us to forget the amazing blessings that we have in our children. We get discouraged. We can focus on the harder, more negative parts of our lives and fail to recognize the treasures which are all around us.

We have entered a time in our home where we are starting to deal with some preteen hormones and conflict. This has recently caused quite a strain on the relationship between myself and my oldest son. I find myself feeling just as impatient and frustrated with his behavior as he seems to be feeling with me. There are days when I question my desire to continue homeschooling him. I figure that if he doesn't want to listen to me anymore, wouldn't it be easier to just ship him off to school and let someone else deal with him?

Then I catch a glimpse of this same son in an old home movie. I see his sweet little face and his smiles and it almost takes my breath away reminding me of the love I have for this child. I miss that little guy sometimes. He can even be a little bit naughty in the movie and it just makes me snicker. It doesn't make me as drop down angry as I seem to get with him nowadays.

And it's even more telling when I see myself on those same old home movies. I'm so encouraging to my little son. I'm so eager to see the new things he's learning. So quick to compliment him and cheer for him when he masters even the most basic skills. When is the last time I've cheered for my son (other than at sporting events?) When is the last time I was eager to come look at something he had created or accomplished?

> *Wouldn't it be easier to just ship him off to school and let someone else deal with him?*

I think I've been way too busy focusing on the wrong things. Yes, it's important to plan and to prepare – but it's also important to enjoy my boys throughout the day. I may have my lessons ready to teach but is my attitude prepared? I want my boys to enjoy learning but am I enjoying teaching? I will be pondering these important questions as I continue to prepare myself for the coming homeschool year.

This year, I want to be their cheerleader as well as their teacher. This year, I want to focus on what's truly important. This year could be the best homeschool year we've ever had if I am able to remember the joy of being a mom to my boys and am able to let go some of the sorrows. I'm truly excited for this year to begin. No one ever said that homeschooling boys would be easy; but, if I can successfully keep the important things in focus, it will be a more joyful journey.

8 Tips for a Tired Homeschool Mom

Parenthood is hard work! Add homeschooling to the mix and us moms definitely have our hands full. So it makes sense that you will be tired from time to time. However, if you find yourself tired all the time – or just plain exhausted – then there are some things you can try to give yourself more energy.

Here are 8 Tips for a Tired Homeschool Mom:

1. Sleep – Are you sleeping well?!? Sleep is important! It's important for our kids and it's also important for us. I've entered a stage of life where I'm not sleeping as well and it has made a huge impact on my energy during the day. In order to get some sleep, I resorted to taking a sleep aid for awhile… until I read a study which said that taking that sleep aid for an extended period of time puts me more at risk for developing dementia!

Now, I'm taking Melatonin, Valerian Root, and a high dose of Chelated Magnesium before going to bed instead. My doctor said that these were all good choices… but that if I still struggle with sleeping after a few weeks that there are things she can prescribe which would be better for me than the over-the-counter sleep aid I was taking before.

Do some research, check with your doctor, and do whatever you can to get your sleeping in order. This will have one of the biggest impacts on your energy level during the day!

2. Food – Are you eating right? This is a hard one for busy moms. We're focused so much on our families that sometimes we don't do what's best for ourselves. Lots of moms grab something quick instead of making wise choices at meal times. Or even worse, sometimes we skip breakfast and/or lunch altogether!

We need good food to fuel our bodies. I have learned this lesson the hard way over and over. When I eat healthy meals and snacks, I feel so much better for it. Junk food tastes good in my mouth – but it doesn't feel good in my stomach. Our kids need healthy food and so do we!

3. Multivitamin – It's pretty much impossible to get all of the nutrients our body needs throughout the day through food. Taking a quality multivitamin is a simple way to be sure you're fueling your body properly.

4. Supplements – There are lots of supplements which can help you to feel more energetic throughout the day.

- **Vitamin D** – Living in Michigan, there are times of the year when it's cloudy and we don't get to see much of the sun. Taking Vitamin D during these times definitely helps to counteract my lethargy.

- **Chelated Magnesium** – This is required for over 300 biochemical reactions throughout the day including turning glucose into energy. If you're feeling tired, you may have a slight magnesium deficiency. Women need 300mg a day and men need 350mg. Take this at night because it helps you to sleep! By the way, I tried taking regular magnesium for awhile but I found that it caused my heart to beat irregularly. Chelated magnesium doesn't do this.

- **L-Tyrosine** – This is an amino acid which can help to counteract stress. If you're feeling stressed on a regular basis, you will also feel tired because your body has a finite amount of chemicals which help us to combat it. L-Tyrosine produces adrenaline and dopamine which helps to protect us from stress.

Again, you should check with your doctor if you want to add supplements to your diet. She may have some great ideas for you to try for your specific situation.

5. Drink water – Did you know that if you are slightly dehydrated that will make you feel lethargic? Drink a tall, cool glass of water and see if your energy level picks up. Our bodies require a lot more water than they usually get. Aim to drink half as many ounces as the number of pounds you weigh. For example, if you weigh 150lbs then attempt to drink 75oz of water each day.

6. Check with your doctor – If you're tired in the morning even after a good night's sleep, you should check with your doctor. She can do a simple blood test to see if your thyroid is functioning properly and to check for anemia. Thyroid function often goes down after childbirth and also during perimenopause. I have hypothyroidism and I'm grateful for the medication which helps me to be less tired!

7. Exercise – Yes, exercise helps us all to feel more energetic. I'm not advocating crazy amounts of exercise – but taking a 20 or 30 minute walk every day or so will help to increase your energy level. Whenever I get out of the habit of taking walks I definitely feel the difference.

8. Take time for yourself – When we're busy we tend to drop everything we're doing for ourselves. As homeschoolers, we're quite often so focused on our kids and on their education that we rarely make any time for activities that we enjoy.

It's important to try to carve out a little bit of time so that you can revive yourself on occasion. Read a book for pleasure, paint a picture, go for a walk, take a bubble bath, or engage in some other leisure activity which can help you to recharge your batteries. This is especially important if you are in introvert! Ask your spouse or a close friend to help keep you accountable in this area.

Are We Frustrating Our Children?

When we first decide to homeschool our children, most of us are excited about the prospect. Yes, there is also some fear that comes with the decision, but mainly we are thrilled that we will be able to teach our children using learning methods which are beneficial for each unique child.

Somewhere along the way, however, the thrill of allowing our children to be themselves somehow turns into frustration. We forget that we initially wanted to provide a customized education for our child and instead we put expectations on our children that don't fit them in any way. We begin to be more concerned with how our children make us look than what's going on in their heart.

Carol Barnier, author of several wonderful books such as ***How to Get Your Child Off of the Refrigerator*** [86], ***On to Learning***[87], and ***The Big What Now Book of Learning***

---

[86] How to Get Your Child Off of the Refrigerator by Carol Barnier
[87] On to Learning by Carol Barnier

Styles[88] has some amazing advice in this area. I had the privilege of hearing her speech called "Don't Miss the Gift in this Child." The following are insights Carol gave on how we go wrong and how to start seeing the gift in our own children.

Where Did We Go Wrong?

Sometimes the problem is that we have the wrong set of expectations for our children. We want them to look and walk and talk like everyone else and when that doesn't happen we become frustrated with them.
Carol encouraged us to think of David in the Bible. When David was preparing to meet Goliath in the battlefield, King Saul attempted to put his own armor on David. The armor was too big for David and he couldn't even walk with it on. David was wise enough to remove Saul's armor so that he could then do the task that God had set before him.

If we try to load our children down with our expectations for them, will they be mature enough to recognize that the armor is merely too big and heavy? Or will they think that they don't measure up? We can cripple our children with discouragement when we expect the wrong things from them.

Sometimes the problem is that we are with our children 24 hours a day, 7 days a week. When we are together this much, it's easy to start focusing on the annoying aspects of each other's behavior as opposed to appreciating the good in our children.

---

[88] The Big What Now Book of Learning Styles by Carol Barnier

It's easy to lose God's vision for them when we are focused on the bad.

What This Can Do To Our Children

When we fall into this trap, we can cause our children to think poorly of themselves. They can come to think that all they are good for is to frustrate us! Children have a tendency to take responsibility for everything that is going wrong in a home. They will take ownership of any misery that you or your family is going through. If this sounds too familiar, it is not too late to turn things around.

> *We can cripple our children with discouragement when we expect the wrong things from them.*

Here are some quick tips for helping your child to realize how important they are to you:

- **Give good apologies, not sermons.** Tell your child you are sorry for your behavior and don't go on to explain it away by blaming them for your reaction.

- **Ask for forgiveness.** Children are eager to forgive us. They love us and want to have a close relationship with us. Be quick to ask for forgiveness when you mess up.

- **Change your future behavior.** Ask your children if you have hurt them in any way that they could tell you. Apologize and then resolve to treat them differently in the future. Each child is different and what is fine with one child may be hurtful to another.

So, how do we start seeing the gift in our child? Here are 8 ways:

- **Pitch Ozzie and Harriet** – we've already talked about having unrealistic expectations for our children. Don't do it. All children are different and we need to appreciate them for who they are.

- **Pitch Wonder Woman** – Homeschooling is a full-time job. You cannot expect to homeschool your children and not give up a few other activities that other moms may be able to perform.

- **Embrace the mess** - Don't expect your home to be neat and orderly at all times.

- **Just say "no"** - Don't think that you will be able to juggle as many church responsibilities as you did in the past. You will have to learn how to say "no."

- **Put down that book** - Reading for pleasure will be something that you do in short spurts if you don't have to give it up altogether during the school year. It is important to take some time for yourself throughout the day – but putting your feet up and reading for 4 hours is probably not going to fit into this season of your life very often.

- **Get a grip** - Keep your "To Do" lists short so that you don't get discouraged. Be realistic about what you can fit into your day.

- **Pitch Dick and Jane** – Don't expect each of your children to be visual learners. Traditional teaching methods expect all children to catch on to one way of teaching and that won't necessarily be the case for your child. Your child may learn better while moving, with hands-on activities, or by listening to their lessons on tape. You may even have to pitch the curriculum that worked for their older sibling and buy something totally different (egads!)

- **See your child the way God sees him** – God doesn't only see our children as they are now, but also as the man or woman that they will become. Be sure to look beyond today with your kids. Just because they struggle with impulse control today doesn't mean that they will struggle with that in a few years. God has a specific plan for your child and it is wonderful!

Concrete Ways to See our Children's Gifts:

- **Be sure to have a consistent quiet time with God** – This can be a tough one with our busy schedules. It is definitely worth it. None of us have the strength to do this momentous task of raising and discipling our children without God's help. Carol says that she doesn't start brewing her coffee until after her Bible is open and she's ready to start her devotions. You may also have to get up a few minutes earlier in the morning to fit this into your day. Do it! You won't be sorry.

- **Write down all of your child's qualities** – Be sure to write down the good and the bad. You and your husband should ponder these qualities and try to discern what God might want your child to become someday. This will help you as you are trying to make decisions that affect your child's education.

- **Try to focus on the positive** – All children have strengths and weaknesses, just as we do. Try to think of those traits that you have previously viewed as negative in a more positive light. For instance, a shy child could also be seen as being tenderhearted or empathetic.

Are we frustrating our children? We need to remember that these children are gifts from God and that they are only being lent to us for a season. See the gift in your child and recapture the joy that you initially felt when you started your homeschooling journey.

Are You Discouraged?

One day, I drove my 13-year-old son to the store to buy him a new pair of shoes. He had been growing so much that it was hard to keep him in clothes and shoes at that age. He was 6'1" and wasn't anywhere near done growing at that point.

We talked as we drove to the store. He sat in the front seat next to me and we had an enjoyable conversation. He told me about something he had been thinking about for awhile. He asked me some questions. His tone of voice was calm and pleasant. It was a joy to be able to spend time with him like that.

It may seem like a small thing; but, this was a big deal to me because my son and I hadn't been getting along very well. As he went through the tween and early teen years, our relationship became more and more bristly. When he was younger, we would have long conversations that never seemed to end.

As my son entered his tween years, however, he didn't want to talk to me as much. He didn't want to spend as much time with our family at all. He started talking fondly about the day when he would move out of the house. Some of the things he said were cutting to my heart.

Are You Discouraged?

I thought that our decision to homeschool our boys would spare us from some of the less pleasant aspects of the teen years. I've heard so many stories of homeschool families who are extremely close… who have deep, meaningful relationships which never seem to get tested… whose children exhibit exemplary behavior at all times… who feel completely fulfilled and never question that what they're doing is working – or at least this is the way it seems from the outside. I wanted that for our family as well.

As my son approached his teens, our home wasn't anywhere near as peaceful and idyllic as I would like. I grew up in a home which was filled with anger and yelling and bitterness and I don't want that kind of thing in my home at all. When your teenage son is yelling at you for the umpteenth time that day, however, it makes it hard to remain calm and loving and peaceful.

> *As my son approached his teens, our home wasn't anywhere near as peaceful and idyllic as I would like.*

Those next several years were much harder than I had anticipated. Does that mean that every moment was terrible? Absolutely not. And I needed to remember that when we were going through a hard moment. But the hard moments were PAINFUL and they took a lot out of me.

I recently saw a video clip by Todd Wilson, the Familyman, called "Lies Homeschooling Moms Believe." In this video, Todd said that homeschool moms end up feeling discouraged much of the time because we think that everyone else has smarter kids, cleaner homes, more elaborate meals, etc.

He also said that many of us feel like we are failing when it comes to teaching our kids. Believe me, I've had days (months?) where I have felt that way as well. It was encouraging to me to think that I wasn't the only homeschool mom to feel this self doubt.

As my boys get older, it often feels like we are at the base of the last steep hill that we have to climb in order to launch our sons into the world. I have SO MUCH MORE to learn – but I will try to share any insights we are able to gain as we navigate through this complex time of life.

Meanwhile, here are a few things which seem to be helping us right now:

1. Pray, Pray, Pray – I don't have all the answers. I definitely need God's wisdom to make it through this phase of life. God has promised that He will give us wisdom if we ask and I'm counting on that!

2. Spend Time with Each Child Alone – My sons act different when they are alone with my husband or I than when we're all together. Whether this is when we tuck them in at night or driving in the car, we need to try to be intentional about finding this alone time with each child.

You may find that these opportunities often come when you are tired or are in a hurry. Slow down and take a few moments to connect with your child – no matter how exhausted you may be feeling at the time. These are the good moments that you will always remember… and so will they.

3. Be Sure they are Getting Enough Rest – All children need plenty of sleep. As teenagers, they still require MORE than 8 hours of sleep a night. Do everything you can to ensure that your kids are keeping a consistent bedtime as often as possible. If you find that your son is struggling more than normal, you may want to schedule lighter studies for that day or even have him do some reading in his room. We've done this before and had my son fall asleep and take a nap for several hours! Getting enough sleep definitely brightens their moods.

> *You may find that these opportunities often come when you are tired or are in a hurry.*

4. **Investigate Supplements** – My oldest son is a terrible eater. He suffers from sensory processing issues and one result of that is that his diet isn't the most balanced no matter how hard I try. After hearing Dianne Craft speak about a boy's brain and how nutritional deficiencies can affect their behavior, we put our boys on a strict regimen of supplements including things like fish oil, probiotics, and 5-HTP. If my boys skipped these supplements for even one day I could tell the difference. (I talk about this subject in detail in the chapter called "Is Your Son's Brain Starving?")

5. Limit Electronics – We were adamant that we weren't going to let our sons get addicted to electronics… but, I was duped into letting them into our home when the Wii came out. I thought the Wii would be different because you supposedly had to move in order to play it. That is so untrue! If your sons aren't yet addicted to video games, think long and hard about even letting them start. We're still trying to figure out how to wean our boys off of these… but they are definitely more surly after they have been staring at a screen for awhile. I think it's because those games are so easy and satisfying that they make real life seem hard in comparison.

6. Spend Time Recharging – Sometimes you just need to get away from the kids and from homeschooling for a few hours. This becomes easier to do as the kids get older and can stay home alone. Try to plan some errand running on your own so that you can enjoy the quiet car. Bring some tea with you and make it into a pleasant, peaceful experience. Schedule some time with friends occasionally. Take a bubble bath. Read a book for pleasure. We all have things we enjoy doing which help us to feel more energized. Try sprinkling a few of these things throughout your week and you will notice a big difference in your own energy level and attitude.

7. Spend Time Alone with Your Husband – This is another thing that we've been trying to do more and it definitely makes a difference. Talk things out with your spouse. Get his feedback. He remembers what it felt like to be a teenage boy. Ask for his advice. Also, just spend some time together without focusing on the kids at all. When your relationship with your husband is good any issues with the kids won't feel as insurmountable.

8. Reach Out – It's easy to keep our discouragements bottled up inside ourselves because it's embarrassing to tell anyone else about our struggles. I am part of a small group of ladies who pray with and for each other. As we've gotten to know each other better we've been able to be more honest with each other. It has made such a difference to know that someone else is praying for us – and that other people are struggling with some of these same issues. Don't try to go it alone. Reach out to at least one other homeschool mom or family member whom you can trust.

9. Hang Onto The Good Times – As my boys are getting older, more and more we are given glimpses into activities they enjoy, skills they are good at, ways they've matured, etc. Write these things down in a journal or somewhere that you can keep handy. Then, when you have a rough day with your son, you can read about all of the areas where he has grown and feel encouraged again. And remember, what you are doing is making a HUGE difference in your son's life!

My oldest son's 13th year was one of the most discouraging ones I've ever had. We dealt with health issues in our extended family, business setbacks, and an extremely harsh winter which kept us inside the house way more than normal. Add to that a tween boy and a teen boy who were starting to feel the effects of their raging hormones and none of us was totally sure how to handle it. It made for some long, long, long, days.

But the difficult phases of life will pass and you and your children will be better for it if you persevere. I love this quote from Scott Brooks, who was a professional basketball player and is now the coach of the Oklahoma City Thunder,

"I believe this with all my heart: the greatest coach of all time in my eyes is my mom. She's instilled in me a toughness and a perseverance and just a never-quit mentality, and I thank her every day for providing for me, for what she sacrificed her life for."

Imagine a day in the future when our sons are able to look back and say something similar about us. Our determination to continue on regardless of the sacrifice and hardships will be inspiring to our children. This is hard, and sometimes it's discouraging; but, we can do it! We must persevere for the sake of our children, our families, and our own personal growth.

Attention Perfect Homeschooling Moms

Are you trying to give your child the perfect education or the perfect homeschooling experience? Are you trying to be a perfect homeschooling mom?

If you think about this logically you'll know that this isn't possible. In our hearts, however, us parents want to do the best we can for our children and do the most we possibly can for our children... and we often beat ourselves up when we fall short.

Relax! You are not perfect and God doesn't expect you to try to be perfect. Us moms, especially, need to cut ourselves some slack. The memories your children keep the longest won't necessarily be WHAT you did with them but WHAT KIND OF ATTITUDE you did it with. If you are stressed because you feel you aren't measuring up, that will negatively affect your child more than if you aren't teaching a lesson well.

Having chosen to homeschool, you may find that your house stays messier and your laundry never quite gets put away. If this stresses you out, you need to remember what's really important in life. When you're on your deathbed, will you regret that you didn't keep your house cleaner? Or will you regret that you didn't enjoy the time you had with your kids because you were stressed out about not feeling like you were measuring up.

If you find yourself stressed out and feeling like you don't measure up, remember the following:

- **You Need to Take Occasional Breaks** – We recently went on a family camping trip. My husband and my sons went off by themselves fishing several times. They absolutely loved it! When they were fishing, I stayed back at the campsite and read a good book. Our boys discovered that they LOVE to fish, so I got a lot more reading time in than I thought I would as well. I felt so recharged after that trip, having had some long overdue time to myself.

The memories your children keep the longest won't be WHAT you did with them but WHAT KIND OF ATTITUDE you did it with.

- **Accept Help from Others** – You can't do it all. You may think that since you're home all day you should be able to run the entire household singlehandedly. Homeschooling is a full time job. You will need to ask for help from your husband and kids in order to get everything done. If you are fortunate enough to have grandparents nearby, be sure to enlist their help as well.

- **You Are NOT Perfect** – Don't expect perfection from yourself or from others. No one is capable of being perfect!

- **Be Flexible** – Things won't always (ever?) go according to your plans. That's alright. You must be flexible and adapt to your current situation. Remember, some of the best homeschooling lessons for you AND for your kids are when things go off plan and are spontaneous.

A book which you may find helpful is called ***Lies Homeschooling Moms Believe***[89] by Todd Wilson. Todd explains how all homeschool moms feel like they are doing a terrible job. Seriously! Why do we all feel like we are failing? Quite often, it is because we are burned out, discouraged, or experiencing overload.

Try to enjoy your role as homeschooling wife and mother! And be flexible. If you can adapt to changing circumstances and stop sweating the small stuff, you and your family will end up on top, no matter what comes your way.

---

[89] Lies Homeschooling Moms Believe by Todd Wilson

De-stressing 101 for Homeschool Moms

Homeschooling is hard work. Yes, it's a blessing. Yes, we enjoy it. But it is also a difficult job and one that can be extremely stressful if we let it. There is the constant concern that we aren't doing enough or that our children are behind in some way. There is almost no alone time in which we can gather our thoughts. The house is harder to maintain because the kids are home messing it up all day long. It's like being a first year teacher for multiple grades... and we do it over and over, year after year.

Being a mom can be stressful in itself; but, being a homeschool mom increases our stress load exponentially... especially on those days when nothing seems to go right and we feel incredibly behind. De-stressing is essential!

So, what can we do to decrease our stress load? Here are some tips:

1. **Have a Back-up Plan** – We know there will be bad days. When this happens, know in advance how you'd like to handle it. When your best laid plans go haywire, how can you recover well? Try to have a field trip idea or a super fun lesson waiting in

the wings for you to pull out and spring onto your children. Sometimes just a change of scenery or plans will help to get everyone back on track.

2. Make a List – Once you're feeling stressed out it can be hard to think clearly. Think of five or ten relaxing things that you enjoy doing and write them down. Try to fit some of these things into your schedule on a regular basis. If you don't have the time to enjoy them often, at least keep the list handy for when you feel the tell tale signs of being stressed out. Be sure to share this list with your husband so that he has ideas to suggest to you when he sees you are overwhelmed. He will probably notice that you are feeling out of sorts before you do.

3. Take a Lunch Break – We all need a few minutes alone each day in order to maintain our sanity. If our children are young, we need to take time for ourselves while they are napping. If they are older, we can train them to read books or play outside or engage in quiet activities while we take a break. Train the children to leave you alone during this half hour or hour of time. If your kids are old enough to be left alone, you might want to consider taking a walk by yourself. These few moments of silent time, where demands aren't being made on you, will go a long way toward decreasing your stress level.

4. **Ask for Help** – The quickest way to burn out is to attempt to do everything on your own. Ask your spouse to pitch in and help out with certain aspects of homeschooling. Ask the grandparents to take the kids and give you a break. Ask another homeschooling mom to swap childcare duties with you so you have a chance to run errands on your own. Ask your family to pitch in with more of the household chores. Some of us are

blessed enough to have people who ask how they can help. Most of us, however, will need to ask people to help. Don't be afraid to ask! People don't know we could use help unless we tell them.

5. Stop Comparing Yourself or Your Children to Others – Everyone is different. Our children are all unique and we are unique as well. Our homeschooling experiences, while similar, will not be exactly the same as anyone else's. Some families will excel in areas in which we struggle. Some will spend time doing many things that don't even hit our radar. That's alright. We all have different priorities, different reasons for homeschooling, different strengths and different children. We need to stop comparing ourselves to other families and run our own, individual races.

Most of us will need to ask people to help.

6. **Consider Joining a Co-op** – Some subjects, such as gym, are hard to teach at home. There are many homeschool co-ops all over the world which offer various types of classes and activities. You may want to investigate the ones near you and evaluate whether or not it would be good for your family to join one. Over the years, we have occasionally been part of a co-op which met on Friday mornings every other week. The cost was minimal and the fellowship was great – for myself and for my sons. Having an outlet where we can visit with other homeschool moms on a regular basis can be positive.

7. **Enroll Your Children in a Class or Extra-Curricular Activity** – There are many different opportunities for homeschool children. You may want to consider finding one

where you can drop your children off at various times to give you a chance to be alone or to run errands on your own. We have found several awesome opportunities such as hands-on science classes and nature classes. These programs have given my boys a chance to learn from someone else. They've also given me a chance to catch up on writing my newsletters and such. We've enjoyed these opportunities when they present themselves.

8. Join a Support Group – This is another great way to fellowship with other homeschool moms. If you join a support group, be sure you come away from it feeling energized and encouraged rather than feeling like you've just attended a complaining or comparing fest.

Being a homeschool mom can be quite stressful. With a little bit of thought and preparation, however, it can be an enjoyable journey in which us moms and our children can benefit immensely over the long run.

Homeschool: Am I Doing Enough?

One of the biggest fears us homeschool moms have is that we aren't doing enough for our kids – or that we aren't making the right decisions for our kids.

We torment ourselves with these questions:

- What if I ruin my son?
- What if he is never able to support a family?
- What if I fail?

At times, I struggle with these questions as well. Taking on the complete responsibility for educating our children is an immense task… and it puts a lot of pressure on us moms. Many of us struggle with the fear that our sons will suffer from our decision to homeschool them.

Am I Making the Right Decisions?

Our family makes a point of attending our state homeschool convention every year. My boys have always enjoyed going to the kids' portions of the conferences. When they were young, they attended the Children's Convention which is run much like a VBS. Every year they would have a ton of fun and make some good friends.

As my boys got older, they had the opportunity to attend classes for tween kids, where they were able to learn about fun stuff like writing and film making. These classes have also been fun and exciting for my boys. And everywhere they went, they enjoyed meeting new kids and learning new things.

When my oldest son turned 13, however, the conference was going to be different for our family. As a teenager, there were going to be even more opportunities for our son. He had the option to either attend leadership training or to be part of the Teen Task Force.

The leadership training sounded like an incredible experience. As soon as I read the description of the training, I was super excited for him. I knew it could be a wonderful learning opportunity. It seemed to fit his strengths perfectly!

The Teen Task Force, on the other hand, does behind the scenes work for the conference. They do all sorts of tasks such as helping to set up and tear down the used book sale, registering people for the conference, and so on. They are a valuable part of the conference; however, I was sure my son would see the value in the leadership training, as I did, and would be eager for me to sign him up.

Imagine my surprise when my son actually wanted to be part of the Teen Task Force! This was the son who needed to be pushed to do his chores every day... the son who only reluctantly went out of his way to help others. He wanted to volunteer at the conference rather than getting something for himself?!?

Of course, you probably can probably guess that this volunteer experience ended up being amazing for my son. I could have sworn that he grew two inches that weekend from having a sense of pride in his hard work. I also learned a lot from watching my son that weekend.

Here are 6 things I learned from my son being a Teen Task Force member:

1. My son CAN take orders!
2. My son IS a hard worker
3. My son IS responsible
4. My son DOES want to help others
5. My son DOES know how to move quickly when necessary
6. I don't always know what's best

I thought for sure my son was making a mistake when he chose a different opportunity than the one I thought would be best for him. I was wrong.

That's alright, though. God had my back! We don't have to put so much pressure on ourselves to be sure we are doing everything our boys need in order to be prepared for life. God will be sure they're ready.

I heard Todd Wilson speak at a homeschool conference a few years ago and he talked about this very thing. He told us the story about how one of his sons grew up to be a biologist – even though he had never been taught any biology during his homeschool years.

Todd said that homeschooling our kids is like planting seeds in a garden. When you plant a pumpkin seed, you always have a pumpkin plant come up. When you plant a bean seed, you always have a bean plant come up. You never plant a zucchini seed only to have a pepper plant come up.

Our kids are who they are. God has made them who they are for a specific purpose. No matter what we do or don't teach them, they will become that person. No matter what experiences they do or don't have, they will become that person.

Are you doing enough?

That was a huge relief to me. We need to remember that God is in control – and that He will ensure my sons receive the teaching and training they need to become the men He wants them to be. Remembering this took a tremendous burden off of my shoulders.

> *"If any of you lacks wisdom, he should ask God, who gives generously to all without finding fault, and it will be given to him." -James 1:5*

God promises He will give us wisdom if we ask. When I feel insecure about homeschooling my boys, I try to remember to take it to God. When I do, He either comforts me… or gives me a nudge in a different direction.

I've had times when I've felt like I needed to talk to my boys about how things were going… and listen to their thoughts. At various times, I've felt like I needed to come up with more opportunities for my boys to socialize with different groups of people. I've gotten bad feelings about certain curriculum we've been working with and have felt like we needed to switch.

Sometimes God will speak to us and will let us know how we need to homeschool. Sometimes He will speak to our husbands. And sometimes God will speak directly to our sons. As long as we are listening for His leading, we have nothing to fear.

"For the Spirit God gave us does not make us timid, but gives us power, love and self-discipline." – 2 Timothy 1:7

Relax, homeschool mom. You aren't alone on this homeschool journey. God wants to guide you through it!

Is Homeschooling Strengthening Your Marriage ?

Or Destroying it?

When my husband and I celebrate our wedding anniversary each year, we always make it a point to ship our boys off to their grandparents' house for a long weekend. (BTW – my husband's parents live right next door to us so they aren't shipped away very far. LOL)

Some years, we are able to afford a romantic getaway. Most years, we have the house to ourselves and we're able to relax, reconnect, and just be together.

We look forward to these anniversary weekends all year long. As parents, the majority of our energy is expended in doing things with and for our boys.

Don't get me wrong – we enjoy this time. Being parents has been one of the best things we've ever done. Being homeschooling parents, however, can be all consuming. It seems like there is a never ending list of tasks which need to be accomplished and which take up the majority of our attention. It isn't often that we're able to sit around and stare into each others' eyes anymore. I'm not sure we ever did that, but I hope you get my point.

Homeschooling can be hard on a marriage. In her book ***The Busy Homeschool Mom's Guide to Romance***[90], Heidi St. John says that many homeschool moms enter a homeschool vortex where their days are filled with "children, curriculum, and crock pots." Often times, we can get so wrapped up in our children and their education that there isn't much room left for thinking about and doing things for our husbands.

> *It isn't often that we're able to sit around and stare into each others' eyes anymore.*

Is homeschooling destroying your marriage?

Our husbands don't want to have to compete with our children for attention. They want to be that special someone who we prefer over all others.

How can you tell if homeschooling is destroying your marriage? Here are 6 things to consider:

1. Are you so busy with lessons that you can't answer your husband's phone calls?

---

[90] The Busy Homeschool Mom's Guide to Romance by Heidi St. John

2. Do you regularly turn down requests for intimacy from your husband because you're too tired?

3. Have you filled up your calendar with events for the children without leaving any white space for time with your husband?

4. Have you lost interest in dating your husband or in talking with him?

5. Have you stopped cleaning yourself up and getting cute for when your husband comes home from work?

6. When your husband walks in the door, do you continue with whatever you're doing or stop to greet him with a hug and a kiss?

It's easy to get a "homeschool headache," as Heidi calls it. This is where we feel that if one more person asks us to do something for him or her we're going to scream. Ask yourself how often your husband has been that person. Are you so burned out at the end of the day that you aren't there for him when he needs you?

Fortunately, if you find yourself in this situation here are three steps you can take for strengthening your marriage:

First, be honest with your husband. Tell him how you're feeling. Be sure he understands that you want to be there for him but you're feeling burned out. Be ready to accept any help or advice that he might want to offer at this point.

Next, make your husband a priority again. Be willing to put on makeup and dress cute for him again. Make the effort to set up dates with him. Build enough margin into your day that you will have some energy and pleasantness left for your husband once he gets home. Don't always make your husband pursue you. Sometimes, he also would like to feel wanted by you.

Finally, remember that these homeschool years really do go by quickly. Make it a point to enjoy this time with your kids and your husband. And remember that someday the kids will leave the house and you and your husband will be alone. Be sure to make your marriage a priority so that when this time comes, you will have a strong, vital relationship to enjoy for many years to come.

One of the biggest benefits of homeschooling is that it is flexible. If you need more time in the afternoon to shower and prepare for your husband's arrival, then take it. Schedule that time if you need to! A strong bond between you and your spouse is one of the best gifts that you can give to your children.

Unfortunately, our family has personally known several Christian homeschooling marriages which have ended in divorce. How sad! Please don't let your marriage become a sad statistic.

Fortunately, homeschooling can also strengthen our marriages and our families.

Homeschoolers have more time to spend at night and on weekends as a family versus having to complete piles of homework. They can enjoy exploring various topics together.

Homeschooling our kids can and should be an amazing family adventure.

Remember your husband. Be intentional about spending time with him! With a little bit of effort and planning, you can strengthen your relationship and have a marriage that will stand the test of time… and of homeschooling!

Keeping Your Sanity in a Busy Homeschool World

If you have been homeschooling for any length of time, you have probably come to the conclusion that you can't keep up with everything the way you would like. You can't volunteer for every position at church. You can't teach every co-op class. You can't keep your home spotless and your yard neatly mowed and trimmed, etc and still have time to properly educate your children. At least you can't do all of these items at the same time and maintain any semblance of sanity!

Does being a homeschooler mean that everything else needs to fall by the wayside? By no means! Many homeschool moms are excellent at juggling multiple responsibilities. We are either born with this talent naturally or we develop it quickly by necessity. Either way, it is possible to homeschool your children and keep up with at least some other responsibilities as well.

How do you do this? Here are several tips for keeping your sanity:

1. **Set Your Priorities** – It is extremely important that you and your spouse be on the same page when it comes to what is and is not a priority. You can waste a lot of time working on less important tasks which will use up time you should have used getting something more vital done.

Sit down with your spouse and come up with a list of all of your projects and responsibilities. Together, you need to decide what is the most important for your family. Obviously, the education of your children is going to be near the top of your list. Other items which may interfere with their education may need to be reconsidered – or you may need to come up with some clever solutions for getting those tasks completed without cutting into your school day.

If you have the financial means, you could always hire some help. If you don't, you could enlist the help of other homeschool moms by swapping responsibilities. One idea would be to have someone else watch your children, teach a specific subject for which they have expertise, or do some other task for which you don't have the time or ability. If you go this route, you will obviously need to reciprocate for her in some way.

2. **Learn to Be Selective** – When you decide to homeschool your children, you will no longer be able to be the Go To person for everyone. You will still be able to volunteer in some capacities and to lend a helping hand to your neighbors and friends. You will, however, need to be more selective about what extra

responsibilities you will be able to take on during this busy season of life.

I used to feel that if I heard about a need, it was my responsibility to try to fill it. I no longer feel this way. I'm learning that there are other people who are willing to help out and my stepping back gives them the opportunity to be able to learn how to step forward and bless people as well.

There are plenty of opportunities where you will still be able to pitch in and help. Try to find times when your husband and children are already involved in an activity and help during those same times. If your children are part of an Awana group or a co-op or some other such activity, that is the perfect opportunity for you to become involved. You will be driving them to and from the activity anyway. It would be a better use of your time to help out during that same time slot than to volunteer for a completely unrelated task.

3. Take Some Time to Decide – This is related to the previous tip. When you are asked to do something instead of saying "yes" or "no" right away, tell the person you need to think/pray/ask your husband about it before giving an answer. Often, when we are asked to do something we feel put on the spot.

It's hard to say "no" immediately. If we have a chance to consider the request, it enables us to either decline or to say yes with a much better attitude. Be sure it will fit into your already busy schedule before you accept another responsibility.

4. Chore Lists on the Fly – If you want any chance of keeping some order in your house, you need to get the entire family involved. I have tried making chore lists a week at a time but that doesn't always work for us. If I sit down and decide a week in advance what I would like each family member to do, I still find myself doing quite a bit of the unplanned cleaning around the house.

What has worked better for my family is to make a new chore list each morning. I have a master chore list on my computer to which I can refer. I can pull chores from this list each morning. Even better, however, is that I can look around at the house and see what needs to be done right then. I add those tasks to my sons' lists and THEN print them out.

This method has been invaluable for us. Tasks that actually need to get done get done – and I get the help I need around the house instead of the same tasks getting completed by my sons whether they need it or not.

By the way, doing chores on a regular basis is a great experience for your child. It helps him to learn life skills that many kids are no longer being taught. When your child grows up and moves out of the house, you'll have the confidence that he can take care of himself without having to learn how to cook or do the laundry as an adult.

5. Spend Time Developing Your Child's Character – Did I just give you another task to add to your already busy day? Not really. Character development is something you should be working on with your children no matter what else you are doing at the time. When I am feeling stressed or overloaded the last thing I want to have happen is to hear my sons fighting or whining or complaining about some task I've asked them to complete. When we help our children to develop self control in these areas, it will be even easier for us to maintain our sanity under pressure.

How do we help our children to develop self control? We can lecture them, buy ANOTHER curriculum, discipline them, etc. The best way to help them, however, is for us to model self control for them.

Try not to be in such a hurry. Don't expect perfection from yourself or your children. Build extra time into your schedule so you don't have to rush. There are many ways to help everyone have a better chance of maintaining their composure, including yourself.

6. Give Yourself Permission to be Silly – I'm sure you know that laughter is the best medicine. One day, when my son said to me, "Mommy, why don't you ever play with us?" I was shocked. In my mind, I played with my boys all the time. I spent every waking moment with them, educating them, playing board games or educational games with them, feeding them, doing chores like laundry with them… what more did they want?

At first I was extremely confused about what my son meant. Then I watched my husband interact with my boys. He would get on the floor and wrestle with them, make goofy noises and faces with them, run around in the backyard with them, ride bikes with them, etc. I didn't see how what he was doing with them was different than what I did with them until I noticed a huge difference. When they were together they were laughing. My husband wasn't being as serious as I usually was and my sons

ENJOYED that. They love joking around and just spending time with their dad!

The kids don't worry about what is or is not getting checked off of a list. They aren't concerned if the game they are playing relates to this week's history theme. They could care less if the field trip has anything to do with a specific science experiment. They just want to laugh, and have fun, and be together.

Since I've started giving myself permission to be silly along with them, we've been enjoying our time together much more. And amazingly, my stress level has also gone down. So give yourself permission to be goofy with your kids. You'll be so glad that you did!

Remembering What's Important

I have had the privilege of attending many homeschool conventions through the years. I've learned so much valuable information from attending them. They are encouraging to me! I highly recommend you look for conventions in your area and put them in your calendar each year. Many states have conventions in the spring.

These conventions are a time to learn new tips, to be uplifted in your homeschooling journey, and to peruse the various vendors who are always on hand. Don't discount this last point. With so many curriculum options in front of you, it is always helpful to be able to touch and look at materials you are considering using before you buy them.

Living Books

One of my favorite speakers that I've heard at a past convention is Sally Clarkson. Her approach to homeschooling is so refreshing to me. In her talk, Sally said that if you aren't enjoying homeschooling then your kids aren't enjoying homeschooling. This is so true! It is important that in our zest for educating our children, we don't lose sight of the reasons why we are educating them at home in the first place.

Sally said that no one will ever be able to teach your kids everything they will ever need to know in life. Our goal should be to give them a love for learning so that throughout their lives they will be able to learn whatever it is that they need to know.

> *If you aren't enjoying homeschooling then your kids aren't enjoying homeschooling.*

Sally's approach to homeschooling resonated with me. She said that educating our children isn't a formula, it's a lifestyle. And that lifestyle needs to be filled with great literature.

She also said that when our children are reading or being read to, their brains are being stimulated and exercised. Thoughts are processed, information is passed back and forth, and their entire brain is being utilized. When our children are sleeping, their brains are in a relaxed state and not much is happening. There is just occasional information flowing as they dream.

Sally said that when our children are playing video games or watching TV, their brains are doing LESS than when they are sleeping. That point shocked me. Everyone knows that video games and TV aren't a great use of time for kids… but I didn't realize that while in these pursuits their brains are more passive than when they sleep?!?

Sally emphasized the importance of having family dinners at the table, where conversation can flow between family members. She recommended that families don't eat in front of the TV. She also said we should try to incorporate family reading times into our nighttime routines as opposed to watching TV together.

This is common sense advice, but it was good to reaffirm what is important. I had been feeling guilty for spending so much time reading with my children – because it was taking time away from math and spelling and some other subjects that were important but not as enjoyable to us.

Sally's lecture encouraged me that it is important to spend that time reading with my children. She said that not only should I NOT feel guilty about it – rather, that I should make even more time for it.

You can read more about Sally Clarkson and her philosophy of education and life in the following books:

- *The Mission of Motherhood*[91]
- *Seasons of a Mother's Heart*[92]
- *Educating the Wholehearted Child*[93]

Try starting your homeschool day by reading aloud to your kids. My boys like to eat their breakfast while I read to them. We've found that this is a relaxing and enjoyable way to start our day!

---

[91] The Mission of Motherhood by Sally Clarkson
[92] Seasons of a Mother's Heart by Sally Clarkson
[93] Educating the Wholehearted Child by Sally Clarkson

You Can't Have It All

You can't have it all... at least not at the same time. I'm not sure who first started selling us the lie that we could have it all... but in modern society that lie is all around us.

We see pictures of smiling fathers traveling all over the world for their jobs – with no sign of the fact that they are desperately missing their families back at home. People post Facebook photos of the beautifully decorated interiors of our homes – even though they only look like that briefly before company arrives. We pin Pinterest recipes of delicious meals to serve our families – regardless of the fact that most nights we are shoveling food down our kids' throats as fast as possible so we can get them to soccer practice on time.

Let's be brutally honest for a moment. None of us can have it all. There are choices to make in life. Period. And no matter what choices we make in life, whether good or bad, there are different sets of issues that we will face as a consequence.

I know without a shadow of a doubt that leaving my career as a network administrator in order to stay at home and raise our boys was a good one. With that good decision, however, my husband and I have had to face some less than savory consequences. Along with all of the wonderful benefits of being a stay-at-home mom, there are also some hard things we have had to face.

Money is much, much tighter on one income. Utility bills are higher since the house is occupied all day long. It's difficult for me to have alone time. And the list goes on...

When moms choose to have a career outside of the home, there are also many pros and cons. Their families may have more money to work with – but they have to give up precious time with their children. Decisions have consequences, good and bad, no matter how we choose to live our lives.

> *It means giving up some things in this life in order to impact your children for eternity.*

Choosing to homeschool your children also has a set of consequences that go along with it. Most of the results are wonderful benefits such as getting to spend more time with your children, being able to teach them about God throughout the day, not having them bombarded by peer pressure, no worries about bullying or school violence, being able to save money on clothes (we all know that the homeschool uniform is pajamas and/or athletic pants, right?!?), being able to teach them in whatever way is best for them, etc.

Even though the decision to homeschool your children is a wonderful one to make, it also has some harder issues that you will need to overcome. Living on one income can be challenging.

There's no way to escape your children – you are together all day every day. Your house is guaranteed to be messier because people are home using the rooms all day long.

There is also a lot of guilt associated with being a homeschool mom. You can't blame the teacher or the other kids when your children are acting up or when they are struggling to learn something. Much of your free time is spent making lesson plans, researching curriculum, and reading things so that we can better teach our children.

Homeschooling is such a blessing! I have never regretted our decision for me to quit my job and homeschool our boys. There are days when I wish we had more money or I wish I could sit around for a few hours in the afternoon sipping my mint tea and reading a book for pleasure. It isn't always easy to homeschool – but nothing worthwhile in life is ever easy.

Homeschooling is hard! You will have to give up some things in order to homeschool. You can't have it all. But when it comes down to it, choosing to homeschool is a wonderful decision. It means giving up some things in this life in order to impact your children for eternity.

When you're having a rough day – or a rough year – and you think about throwing in the towel, remember why you chose to homeschool in the first place. Yes, it is a sacrifice. But it's the kind of sacrifice you will never regret having made. If you can't have it all, be sure you are choosing to hang onto what is truly important in this life.

7 MUST DO Homeschool End of Year Tasks

If you're anything like me, you may have a tendency to feel a bit crispy around the edges in the month of May. I've even gotten that feeling in March some years! Sometimes our homeschooling years can feel long... a bit too long even.

Before you hang up your hat for the summer, however, here are 7 MUST DO.

Homeschool End of Year Tasks:

1. Celebrate – This is an easy one for some of us to skip. If we're completely fried at the end of the year, the last thing we want to do is to add something else to our calendar. It's important for us to celebrate the accomplishments of our kiddos, however. Hopefully, they've worked just as hard as you have. A great way to motivate them to continue working hard in the coming years is to give them recognition for a job well done.

Have a graduation ceremony, throw a party, host an open house, consider a grandparents' day so your kids can show off, or go on a vacation or a special field trip. Try to do something memorable to commemorate the end of your homeschooling year.

Even if you continue to do some sort of schoolwork over the summer, you will want to occasionally celebrate your children's accomplishments.

2. Recordkeeping – Right now, you may think you will never forget what your children have done during the year. In a few years, however, I guarantee you won't remember everything.

Here are some of the things you might want to record:

- Subjects studied by each child (including grades, tests, special projects or papers written)
- Books read or listened to (including audio books)
- Movies watched
- Field trips taken
- Extracurricular activities
- Volunteer hours
- Special Awards

It's even more important to keep track of your child's accomplishments if they are in their high school years.

I like to keep track of some of this information each week such as books they are reading. If I don't write these things down as they're doing them, I'll never be able to keep track of them all.

For other things, such as field trips or extracurricular activities, I can simply look back over our calendar at the end of the year.

You may also want to gather some photos of different things your child has done throughout the year. These can be put into a scrapbook or simply stored on a CD or in a folder on your hard drive. It doesn't matter as long as you know where to find them in the future.

3. Evaluate your year – What did you think about your curriculum choices? Should you continue along the same path next year or find something else which might work better? Do you need to consult with other homeschool moms or experts? Do you feel like your child is learning? Can you identify any strong or weak areas for each child?

4. Talk to kids about what they think – Take time to talk to each of your children one-on-one. What did they think about the school year? Do they have any areas of interest they would like to further explore? Are there any changes they'd like to make next year? Are they having any struggles they'd like to discuss?

5. Talk to your spouse – Take all of the information you have gathered and have an end of year conference with your spouse. Tell him about your hopes and fears for each child. Talk about your struggles. Ask for advice. Pray together about any changes you may need to make..

6. Plan for next year – Using your state requirements, the interests of your child, and his learning style, come up with a plan for each child for the coming year. You may want to get a rough idea in place at the beginning of the summer and order any materials you might need. Then, once the next year is a bit closer and you've had a chance to rest, start coming up with a more detailed plan for the coming year.

7. Take a break of some sort – Depending on your homeschooling schedule, you may be gearing up to take the entire summer off. Or you may just take a day or a week here and there throughout the year. There is no one right way to take breaks – but be sure that you take them. It's easy to burn yourself or your kids out if you try to keep on working constantly without ever taking any time off. God created us to work on 6 days and to rest on the 7th. We shouldn't feel guilty about taking occasional breaks.

> *Pray together about any changes you may need to make.*

The years can feel long for homeschooling moms. If we complete the above seven tasks at the end of each year, however, we will have the best possible opportunity to remember what has been accomplished, to evaluate learning, and to craft an amazing coming year for yourself and your kids!

Attend a Homeschool Convention

Depending on where you live, you may or may not have a homeschool convention coming up soon in your area. There are many wonderful homeschool conventions which take place each year. Some of you may never have attended a homeschool convention and aren't sure it would be worth your time. Whether you've attended a convention in the past, or not, I encourage you to try attending one this year.

Here are several reasons why I believe you should attend a homeschool convention:

1. It's Refreshing – It's extremely refreshing to be somewhere with hundreds or even thousands of other homeschoolers. Let's face it, in most areas of life we are viewed as being a little bit different. Even some in our extended families and our church families tend to think we're a bit nutty. Although homeschooling is becoming more popular every year, we're still viewed by many as being a little bit odd.

At a homeschool convention, you will be surrounded by other homeschoolers. You will feel yourself breathe easily as you can be yourself and not have to be ready for attack from well-meaning but misunderstanding people who have a tendency to question our methods and/or our motives.

2. It's Informative – You will glean some new tips. Homeschool conventions offer a variety of workshops taught by some amazing people in the homeschool community. Depending on the size of the convention you attend, you could be taught by national leaders, parents who have homeschooled for 20 years or more, and experts in their field. Be sure to bring a notebook and pen so you can write down and remember some of this valuable advice. It's such a blessing to be able to learn from people who have gone before us.

3. It's Social – Your kids get to meet other homeschooled kids. Many homeschool conventions have a teen option and/or a children's convention that meet at the same time. These opportunities allow your children to make more friends their age in the homeschool community. It's always a highlight of my boys' year when they attend a children's convention. They usually come home with new pen pals every year.

4. It's Special – Spend some special time with your spouse. If you attend with your spouse, homeschool conventions are a great way for you to get back on the same page concerning your children's education. Even if you attend separate workshops, you will be listening to keynote speakers together. It's a great way to get your priorities straight as a couple, to decide what is working with your homeschool, and determine what might need to be changed.

5. It's Thrifty – Shop for curriculum. Usually homeschool conventions have vendors who come and advertise their wares. This is a great way to get a good look at something before you buy it. The vendors usually have special convention prices as well, so you can save a few bucks. And sometimes there is the opportunity to buy used curriculum, saving you even more money!

6. **It's Essential** – Stand up and be counted. The more homeschoolers who attend the conventions, the more our politicians notice. Homeschooling has come so far in the courts and in the eyes of our fellow citizens. We don't want to lose ground and go back to the days when we didn't have the right to educate our own children.

Some homeschoolers outside of America have to deal with persecution even now. Head to at least one homeschool convention in your area and lend strength to the homeschool movement.

7. It's Critical – Learn about important issues. If there is important legislation coming up for a vote in your area, you will learn about it at a homeschool convention. You will be told if you need to contact your congressman about a specific issue. You will be informed about any other grassroots actions which may be beneficial for that situation. This is a good way to stay informed about news which is important to homeschoolers.

It has become a priority for our family to attend two or three of the homeschool conventions in our area each year. If you already make it a point to attend conferences in your area, that's great! If you've never been to one before, I strongly encourage you to give one a try this year, if at all possible. I truly believe you'll be glad you did!

The 5 Dangers of Attending Homeschool Conventions

I love homeschool conventions. In the previous chapter, I wrote about all of the reasons I think all homeschoolers should attend the conventions in their area. I believe there are LOTS of positive reasons for attending.

There are some homeschoolers who avoid going to conventions, however, because there can be some negative aspects to attending them as well.

I feel that the pros outweigh the cons… but there are some dangers associated with attending which you should be aware of before you go.

Here are 5 Dangers of Attending Homeschool Conventions:

1. **Feeling Overwhelmed** – Homeschool conventions can be large and chaotic. If you're new to homeschooling or are attending your first convention, I recommend you look for one which is on the smaller side. The large state-wide conventions

are packed with attendees, vendors, and workshops. This can be a blessing and a curse. While you're there, don't feel like you need to do it all! That's not even possible. Relax and enjoy the experience.

2. Distraction – The vendor halls will be filled with all sorts of deals of which you can and should take advantage. They are also filled with lots of colorful, shiny looking books which can be a huge distraction. Don't feel that you need to rethink your entire plan every year. If your math curriculum is working for your family, simply get the next book in the series. If your kids are benefiting from reading real books versus using a textbook for history, stick with your plan.

> *Don't feel that you need to rethink your entire plan every year.*

Don't allow yourself to be enticed by the beautiful book covers! Go with a list in hand of items you need and try to stick to looking for those items. Even if you do have something new catch your eye that you'd like to consider, don't fall into the trap of trying to change everything at once. Small, incremental changes are best.

3. Comparison – There is no one right way to homeschool. Workshop speakers are there to HELP you… not to make you feel that your homeschooling style is inferior to theirs. Listen for tips which can be beneficial and let the rest go. It's easy to fall into the comparison trap. Don't do it! God has all of our kids on earth for different reasons. He has given your children to you to parent. Trust that He will guide you in your journey and don't be tempted to compare your weaknesses (or your child's weaknesses) with other people's strengths.

4. Pride – You might also be tempted to fall into the opposite trap of feeling prideful of the way you homeschool your kids versus how a workshop speaker, or vendor, or fellow attendee does. Pride is a sin you want to guard against and is just as destructive, if not more so, than is being overly harsh with yourself. Let's give each other the grace to walk our own paths without feeling that we need to stand in judgment of each other.

5. Confusion – Most conventions have a large variety of workshops available that you can attend. These workshops will feature speakers with differing opinions on many topics. Take advantage of the workshops you feel will benefit your family and discard the rest. Sometimes you will hear information which is extremely helpful. Sometimes you will hear information which isn't pertinent to your situation – or which will bog your family down if you attempt to follow it. Pray about any changes you are considering before you make them to be sure these changes are right for you. Don't feel that you need to implement everything you learn. Just because you hear it doesn't mean you need to do it!

There are lots of benefits to attending homeschool conventions; however, there are some pitfalls as well. Armed with the above information, I would highly recommend that you and your family attend a convention in your area. They are filled with a wealth of information – and the camaraderie you can find there with the other homeschoolers is invaluable.

What About Socialization?

Probably the question that new homeschoolers have to answer the most is, 'What about socialization?' Superior test scores have caused people to stop worrying that homeschoolers won't learn necessary academic skills; however, they still worry that homeschoolers won't learn necessary social skills. People hear the word homeschool and socialization is the first thing that pops into their mind.

Now that my boys are older, we don't get this question very often anymore. Friends and family members have seen the fruit of our labors and they don't worry as much about the fate of our boys if we keep them out of school.

They have seen their exceptional character play out in the world around them. They know that our boys are polite. They have seen them go into public places and approach complete strangers to sell Cub Scout popcorn. They have heard how they can and do make friends whenever they go to a park, beach, or playground. They have heard them carry on conversations with adults and kids alike. They have seen them be kind to the younger children around them.

When you are first starting out, however, you can't reassure well-meaning family members and friends by pointing to results in your own children. It can be extremely discouraging to begin this new journey of homeschooling only to be met with negativity by the important people in your life. So what can you do if you are in this situation?

Here are a few things to keep in mind the next time you are asked the socialization question:

- **Socialization in schools is artificial** – Yes, kids who attend public or private school become socialized. This is a false type of socialization, however. Kids are placed in classrooms by age. This is the only time in people's lives when they spend so much time with others who are all the same age. Being in age-segregated classrooms can lead to the students exhibiting childish behavior and disrespect.

- **Socialization in schools can be extremely negative** – Children in public schools are surrounded by violence, drugs, promiscuity, emotional disorders, criminal behavior, contempt for authority, desperate behaviors, and illiteracy. Many of them become extremely peer dependent and begin exhibiting these same behaviors. This is the socialization we want our children to avoid!

- **Publicly schooled children are more likely to have antisocial behaviors** – Dr. Larry Shyers, a highly qualified individual and family counselor, administered the Direct Observation Form of the Child Behavior Checklist in two groups of children for his dissertation: traditionally schooled students and homeschooled students. This checklist identifies 97 different types of problematic behaviors.

The traditionally schooled students exhibited eight times as many antisocial traits as their homeschooled counterparts. Dr. Shyers' dissertation won the national award in excellence in research from the Educational Research Information Clearinghouse (ERIC) in 1992. His research flies in the face of public school advocates who claim that children need to attend school to be properly socialized.

- **You choose who will influence your child** – Students who attend school for the majority of their waking hours are mainly influenced by their peers. Homeschooled students are mainly influenced by their parents. Who would you prefer having as the main influence in your child's life?

- **You choose whose worldview they will be taught** – Some public school advocates feel that all religion has been removed from the classroom; however, this is not the case. Yes, the Christian religion has been removed from the classroom. However, it has been replaced by the religion of secular humanism. When your child attends school, he will be taught subjects from the slant of whatever worldview his teacher or the curriculum portrays. Homeschooled students are taught subjects from the slant of whatever worldview their parents believe. Whose worldview would you rather have your children taught?

Seeing is believing. Some critics will not be satisfied until your children are grown, gainfully employed, and married with children. Others will start to relax once they see your kids begin to develop into mature and confident people. The main thing to remember is that you and your spouse chose to homeschool for reasons that were important to you. Write those reasons down. Think about those things every time someone gives you a hard time about your choice.

Your children have been given to you to raise. You need to do what you feel is right as their parent and let go of any negative comments made by others. Also, try not to take the comments personally – most of the people who make them are misguided but they actually do have good intentions.

Sometimes it isn't easy; but, as you continue down the path and see the progress your children make, you will be so glad you stuck to your convictions and homeschooled them. Your kids will be so much better off because of the time you willingly invested in their lives.

What If the Kids Want to Go Back to School?

Let's say that you've either made the huge decision to remove your kids from school or have decided not to send them in the first place. You have made the commitment to homeschool them and things seem to be going well, in your opinion. What do you do if your kids decide that they want you to put them back?

I have received several questions from parents asking me that question. It can be a heartbreaking position to be in. You've sacrificed, you've planned for hours, week after week. You've dedicated yourself to the task... only to have one or more of your children reject the whole idea. It can be tough when our kids want (or think they want) something different than what we've chosen for them. What is the best thing to do in this situation?

The answer to that question depends on several factors:

- **Age of your children** – The older your children are, the more input they need to have. When children are young, it is important for us to make decisions for them. As they get older, however, they need to start having a say in what happens in their lives.

No matter how old our children are, however, we are their parents. Some decisions still need to be made for them. Quite often, our children aren't going to agree with us and we need to make our case and stick to our convictions. If we do it correctly, with the right intentions, they will thank us for it someday.

- **How strong is your desire?** – Why did you decide to homeschool in the first place? What are your reasons? If these reasons are extremely strong, you should stick to your guns more adamantly than if you just had a mild curiosity about it and wanted to give it a try.

  If you've been in prayer about the decision and feel that homeschooling is God's will for your family, then you need to continue. No matter what your kids' short-term response might be, you want to be fully in the middle of God's plan for your life. Sometimes it's hard to understand why God wants us to go down a certain road in life – but we still need to continue on in that direction. Explain to your kids that God is in control and we need to obey Him, whether we understand Him or not.

- **How strong is their desire?** – We all know that the more children want something the more passionate their responses will be. Is your child just asking mild questions or are they off-the-charts ardent about returning to school?

Remind them that whatever they're remembering is from younger years of school. As they get older and school gets harder, they would have less and less social time with their friends. They would have been sitting at a desk for hours a day – not able to talk or pass notes, unless they wanted to get into trouble. They would have been able to socialize with their friends at lunchtime and recess and that's about it.

You can force your child to be homeschooled but you can't make him learn. If your child is fighting your attempts to homeschool, here are some positive strategies you can use to try to win over their heart:

1. **Make it special** – Every time you do something with them that they wouldn't be able to do if they were in public school, be sure to mention it to them and play it up. For instance, make a big deal about taking off the first warm day in the spring. And emphasize how special it is that your family gets to spend time together in the evenings instead of having to do homework for hours. Be sure they see how late that big, yellow bus goes by in your neighborhood to drop off kids… so that they realize how much LONGER they would be sitting at a desk if they were in school.

Paint a clear picture to your kids about the PROS of homeschooling and the CONS of public school. Yes, there are pros and cons to both – but right now you want to get them to focus on the positive aspects of homeschooling.

2. **Make it enjoyable** – Add in a subject or two about which your kids are especially interested. We've added in computer programming for one son and videography for the other. They

spend time every day doing these extra subjects and it is time that they look forward to. They wouldn't be able to spend time pursuing their own interests or have many options on their educational choices if they were in a traditional school. Be sure they realize this!

3. Make it fun – Be intentional about throwing some fun or joy into your school day. This is always a great thing to do, anyway. But since you're trying to turn their heart toward home, a great way to do that is to laugh together... They think their best childhood memories are at school. Ask them what it is they remember so fondly and try to recreate or top some of those experiences at home. It should be easy to do because you have so much more freedom than does the school.

> *Paint a very clear picture to your kids about the PROS of homeschooling and the CONS of public school.*

4. Connect with friends – If they're missing specific school friends, have them over occasionally. After being away from them for awhile, those friends may have changed in an undesirable way. Your kids might not miss them so badly if they are able to spend time with them again. If they still have common interests, help your child to have time to spend with them. Just because they aren't going to school together doesn't mean they can't continue their friendship. Let him email a friend or have an occasional lunch date with a buddy. Consider letting him talk on the phone or Skype on days when getting together with a friend wouldn't be possible.

5. Teach them about other homeschoolers – Homeschooling isn't the prominent educational model in modern society. However, it used to be! There are many cool people throughout history who were homeschooled and who went on to become famous authors, artists, inventors, business men, presidents, pastors, missionaries, etc. Teach your children about these great men and women. Once they realize what great company they are in, they may accept homeschooling more readily.

6. **Consider a co-op** – It's important to spend time doing activities with other homeschool families. If you don't belong to a co-op you might want to consider that option. We have belonged to one that only met every other Friday morning – but it gave my boys a consistent time when they were able to have a few classes with their homeschool buddies. My boys appreciated that time!

I've also been intentional about setting up field trips and taking off afternoons occasionally to visit with their friends. They've enjoyed that as well. My boys are social and they miss being around other kids if we aren't doing it often enough. Obviously, you need to have balance and still get the schoolwork done – but if you realize you haven't been doing it very often, you might want to bump friend time up a little bit.

7. Join a team – Being on a sports team can help your child fulfill part of their social craving. My boys have played softball, basketball, baseball, and even touch football with various homeschool groups and that has been another fun way for them to make friends, burn off some energy, and have time away from home.

8. Make it real – Have heart-to-heart talks with your kids and explain to them why you're doing what you're doing. Make sure they have a vision for why you are homeschooling. This isn't just a crazy impulse. Homeschooling is important for you and you honestly feel it is the best option for your family or you wouldn't be doing it.

9. Give them input – Be sure you are communicating with your children. Ask them what they miss. Try to incorporate activities they would appreciate throughout your homeschool day. Be sure you are using techniques which appeal to the way they learn best.

10. Engage their minds – Be a student of your child. Teach them in a way that will activate their interest and turn on their love for learning. Throw away as many worksheets as you can. Read them great books. Do active learning activities with them. If your child enjoys learning they aren't going to want to stop!

It can be devastating when our children don't think they want to be homeschooled. Sometimes with a few minor changes to our routine, we can help them to see that homeschooling can give them the freedom to have a specialized education that will be just right for them.

Take the time to talk with your kids and to determine what will work best for your family. Once you've won over your child's heart, you will be able to better enjoy the long days that you spend together. It's definitely worth the effort!

No Money for Vacation?

Great Ideas for Family Fun at Home

Many families live with less money once they decide to homeschool. Our family was cut in half when we decided to have me quit my job. We've had some extremely lean years where our budget has shrunk tremendously. When that happens, extra things such as vacations simply do not fit very often anymore.

Surprisingly, our leanest years have been some of the ones that our family has enjoyed even more time together as a family. As gas prices go up and my husband's salary would shrink, we found many free activities we could do together – many without ever leaving our home.

Ideas for Family Fun at Home:

1. **Campfire in the backyard** – We have a fire pit in our backyard. We've been able to enjoy hours of enjoyment sitting around a fire talking, singing, and enjoying each other's company. Even people with the smallest yards can usually purchase a small chiminea or other outdoor fire pit. Cooking

hotdogs or marshmallows will heighten the experience even further.

2. Pitch a tent in backyard – Campground fees can add up, even if you're camping with a tent. So why not pitch a tent in your backyard? Make it fun by cooking over the fire, hanging up a clothesline to dry swimsuits and towels, and trying not to enter the house very often. You can make the camping experience as authentic as you would like. Go fishing, let the kids run through the sprinkler, sit around in lawn chairs… the sky's the limit.

3. Board games – Remember when we were children and we spent hours playing games with the family? Board games and card games are a great way to have free fun with your family. Most of us have a closet full of games the kids have received as gifts over the years. Dust them off and have a family game night. It's a great way to get to know your children better.

4. Reading aloud – Reading to our children is so important. Having dad read aloud to the family at night can be a wonderful way to spend time together. Choose books which are just above the reading level of your oldest child. Be sure to use expressive voices to make the experience fun.

5. Movie night – You don't have to go to an expensive theater in order to enjoy a movie. Watch a family friendly video together at home. This is a great time to pop some popcorn or make some other yummy treats to enjoy together.

6. Bike rides – One of the tricks to saving money is to use resources we already have versus purchasing new ones. Most families already have bikes which are stored in our garages gathering dust. Get them out and go for a bike ride. Biking is great exercise and family fun at the same time. More and more groups such as Rails to Trails are creating bike paths around the country. Search the internet to find some bike trails near your home.

7. Hikes – We are fortunate to live near some woods, where we can go on nature hikes whenever we'd like. Again, you can search the internet to find hiking trails in your area.

This is just a small sampling of ideas you can try for having fun with your family without breaking the bank. This year, if you can't afford an expensive vacation try some of these inexpensive family activities you can do around home. You may find that your best summer memories are made when you are relaxing at home as a family.

Rewards for Kids

Offer Rewards and Watch their Motivation Soar

You might wonder if rewards for kids are a good idea. There are many parents and educators alike who tend to think of rewards as bribes and they are opposed to handing them out to their children. Dr. James Dobson, founder and chairman of Focus on the Family, has a lot to say on the topic of rewards for kids:

"It is unfortunate, that one of our most effective teaching tools is often rejected because of what I would consider to be a misunderstanding of terms. Our entire society is established on a system of rewards, yet we don't want to apply them where they are needed most: with young children.

As adults, we go to work each day and receive a paycheck every other Friday. Getting out of bed each morning and meeting the requirements of a job are thereby rewarded. Medals are given to brave soldiers, plaques are awarded to successful business people, and watches are presented to retiring employees. Rewards make responsible effort worthwhile.

The main reason for the overwhelming success of capitalism is that hard work and personal discipline are rewarded materially. The great weakness of socialism is the absence of reinforcement; why should a person struggle to achieve if there is nothing special to be gained? This system is a destroyer of motivation, yet some parents seem to feel it is the only way to approach children. They expect little Marvin to carry responsibility simply because it is noble for him to do so. They want him to work and learn and sweat for the sheer joy of personal accomplishment. He isn't going to buy it!"

I definitely agree with Dr. Dobson. I would much rather offer rewards to my children than to have to argue, plead, or punish them. Children need to learn how to behave appropriately, and a positive rewards system can help you in their training.

Student Incentive Ideas for Younger Children:

- Have a rewards basket that they get to choose from when they do an assignment well
- Give them lots of praise
- Stickers are always a treat
- Write their percentage on the top of their papers. Having a large 100% at the top of the page is motivating
- Throw them a circus peanut and have them try to catch it in their mouth
- Let them earn a trophy, plaque, ribbon or certificate
- Take a trip to a video store or movie theater
- Take a trip to a zoo, aquarium, or museum
- Give them a set of flash cards printed from a computer.
- Receive a 'mystery pack' (gift-wrapped items such as a notepad, folder, puzzle, baseball cards, etc.)

- Receive a plant, seeds and a pot for growing
- Earn an item such as a Frisbee, hula hoop, jump rope, paddle ball or sidewalk chalk, which promote physical activity
- Take a trip to the treasure box (non-food items such as water bottles, stickers, key chains, temporary tattoos, yo-yo's, bubbles, spider rings, charms and pencil toppers)
- Receive art supplies, coloring books, glitter, bookmarks, rulers, stencils, stamps, pens, pencils, erasers and other school supplies
- Watch a video
- Read outdoors
- Teach the class
- Get extra art time
- Have more outside play time that day
- Receive verbal praise in front of brothers and sisters
- Enjoy class outdoors
- Throw them a party
- Screen time
- Go on a walking field trip
- Listen to music while working
- Play a favorite game or puzzle
- Eat lunch outdoors
- Dance to favorite music in the classroom
- Earn play money to be used for privileges
- Listen with a headset to an audiobook
- Go to the library to select a book to read
- Allow your child to have a few friends over after school to play sports or watch a movie
- Invite a few of their friends to a sleepover
- Let the child help plan a special outing

- Read a bedtime story of your child's choice
- Have a family game night, and let the child choose the game(s)
- Allow the child to pick a movie that the family will watch together or an outdoor sport that the family will play together
- Keep a box of special toys, computer games or art supplies that can only be used on special occasions

Student Incentive Ideas for Older Children:

- Buying a tape or CD
- Camping out
- Computer time
- Driving the car on a family trip
- Finding a part-time job
- Getting a chance to earn money
- Getting a driver's license
- Getting to sleep in late on the weekend
- Getting a special haircut or hair style
- Getting to stay out late
- Getting to use the family camera
- Going bowling, skating, etc. with friends
- Going horseback riding
- Going shopping with friends
- Going to a concert with friends
- Going to Disneyland or some other amusement park
- Going to summer camp
- Going to the library
- Going to the movies with friends
- Having a date during the week

- Having car privileges
- Having dating privileges
- Having friends over
- Having their own checking account
- Inviting a friend to eat out
- Making a trip alone
- Participating in activities with friends
- Playing the stereo
- Receiving a magazine subscription
- Redecorating their own room
- Selecting something special for dinner
- Selecting TV programs
- Skating or bowling with friends
- Staying up late
- Staying overnight with friends
- Taking dancing or music lessons
- Talking additional time on the telephone
- Taking time off from chores

Try offering some of these rewards to your kids and watch their attitudes and behavior improve. I firmly believe that these student incentive ideas can have a positive impact on your next homeschooling year.

Getting Dads More Involved with Homeschooling

Moms typically bear the brunt of the load when it comes to homeschooling. Dads are away at work all day long, and sometimes even over the weekend, to make ends meet in the mostly one-income families of homeschoolers.

This makes for an interesting problem. How can you get your husband involved in your children's education? Dads may not be home all day, but they are integral to the success of a child's homeschooling experience. This is especially true if you are raising sons. Moms can educate a boy's mind, but a male influence is needed to turn that boy into a man.

You can do many things to help get dads more involved in the homeschooling process. Here are a few ideas:

Spiritual Leadership

God has called dads to be the spiritual leaders of their homes. Dads may not be home while moms are going through the Bible curriculum with their children; however, they can still be the rudder that steers the spiritual direction in their homes.

Dads should help to make the decisions about what Bible topics are covered in their homes. They should have a hand in picking the Bible curriculum, as well as the curriculum for all other topics each year. It can be easy for dads to stand back and let their wives make these decisions on their own. Dads need to resist this tendency. Their wisdom and leading from God is crucial to the process.

> *Moms can educate a boy's mind, but a male influence is needed to turn that boy into a man.*

Dads should do some type of family devotions. They should also oversee their children to be sure that personal devotions are taking place. This type of spiritual guidance and support from our husbands is necessary.

Dads should also set the example when it comes to their personal devotions. Children should see their dads in Bible study and prayer. For boys to take their own devotions seriously, it is vital that they see this example from their fathers. This will make it much less likely that they will walk away from their faith as adults.

Character Building

Much of the focus in our children's education is on filling their minds with information and teaching them how to think. We forget that it is just as important, if not more so, for us to train their character. Honesty, integrity, trustworthiness, generosity, being a good friend... these are all traits that we need to live out in front of our children.

Character lessons are mostly caught – not taught. There are several good programs which can help us to teach character education to our children. If our children don't see us live these qualities out in everyday life, however, the lessons they learn won't stick.

Dads must get in on these kinds of life lessons as well. It is important for both moms and dads to teach their children to live in such a way that all of their actions bring glory to God.

Use scripture to teach these timeless lessons to your children. When our children do things with a bad attitude, remind them of Philippians 2:14, *"Do everything without complaining or arguing."* When they are angry with their sibling or are being unkind, remind them of Ephesians 4:32, *"Be kind and compassionate to one another, forgiving each other, just as in Christ God forgave you."*

Building Projects

Most dads have home improvement projects waiting for them when they get home from work. These projects can be wonderful hands-on learning experiences for kids. If you have young children let them hand you tools as you teach them about their use. As soon as possible, try involving your children even further in the process. Let them pound in nails, use the staple gun, measure things for you, drill holes, etc.

It's also fun to build special projects with your kids. Try your hand at creating go-carts, model airplanes, rockets, kites, swing sets, etc. There are an infinite number of projects you can build together.

As their skills progress, you can have your children help to plan projects, create designs using software on the computer, and attempt building things on their own or with minimal supervision.

The goal is to help your children become proficient and confident when using tools. These types of learning experiences will long be remembered by your children. And their new skills will be valuable to them in everyday life as well.

Handyman Skills

Dads often have repairs they need to make around the house as well. Turn those "Honey Do" lists into learning opportunities by involving your children. Most men wish they knew more about electrical work, plumbing, appliance repair, carpentry, etc. Focus on teaching these types of skills to your children.

> *The goal is to help your children become proficient and confident when using tools.*

If you don't know much about these trades yourself, now is the perfect time to learn. Buy a book on basic home repair. You can also view videos about how to repair just about anything on YouTube.

Remember to start with something small. You may want to learn how to change a faucet or showerhead before you tackle replumbing your whole house. Build a birdhouse with your kids before you attempt to design and build a dining room table.

Your kids don't care if you know everything there is to know about a topic. As long as you have a spirit which is willing to learn and a sense of humor, you can teach your children and learn at the same time.

If you feel more comfortable, hire a professional and watch him make repairs with your children. Ask him to explain things as he does them. Be sure to let the repairman know your intentions before he agrees to the job. Some people will be more open to people watching them work than others.

Reading Aloud

Reading is one of the most important aspects of your child's education. It is important not only for your child to read but also for us to read to him as well.

Most parents read out loud to their children when they are young. As soon as children learn how to read on their own, however, they often stop reading to them. This is a big mistake. It is important that parents continue to read aloud materials which are just above the reading levels of their children. This teaches our kids correct grammatical patterns, gives us quality time together as a family, and is just plain fun.

Get dad involved in reading to the family. Dads are great at adding inflection and using silly voices to bring stories to life.

Also, when sons hear their fathers reading, they are more likely to become readers themselves. If boys only see their moms reading, they can come to the inaccurate conclusion that reading is only for girls.

Choose books which are entertaining both for boys and for girls. There is no point reading aloud books which are dry and won't hold the interest of you or your children. Books with plenty of adventure and humor are great choices for these family reading sessions.

Higher Math, Dissection and Other Gory Items

Moms are usually a bit nervous when it comes to teaching certain school subjects. Calculus may be a good subject to have dads teach. If you are a math wiz but you aren't the best at spelling or history, let your husband take over that subject instead. He can teach it when he gets home from work or after dinner.

Biology is another subject that makes some moms squeamish. To help your husband be successful, moms can help out by organizing the materials for their spouse. Moms can also order the necessary materials and turn them over to dads, who can dissect with the kids after dinner. Mom can also do the bookwork with the kids during the day and dad can simply do the hands-on instruction at night.

However you divide up the tasks, focus on each other's strengths. If dad is an engineer or a computer professional, you will want to capitalize on his knowledge by letting him instruct your children in these areas. If he's a master chef or an orchestra conductor, then it'll be obvious to you what areas he would be best at teaching. The possibilities are endless! Do whatever works for your family.

Internships and Apprenticeships

Many times, dads have more connections to the outside world than do moms, as their jobs usually take them away from their homes every day. Dads can ask other men to mentor their children. If your son is interested in being a doctor, ask a health professional from church if he can tag along on the job.

This kind of real experience is invaluable for kids when they are deciding what it is God wants for their profession. It is one thing to read about being an electrician or an engineer. It is another thing entirely to apprentice under an electrician or to have an internship at an engineering firm.

Look through your church directory to determine the many different professions that are represented there. Talk with people from work to see if they may have connections that could be beneficial to your child's education. Check with extended family members to see if they know someone in a profession that interests your child.

The more real life careers your child is able to experience or observe the better. All of that experience will help him to make more informed decisions when he is choosing a major in college, choosing a trade school, or deciding where to send resumes.

This is just a sampling of some of the ways that dads can be directly involved in their child's education. God intentionally placed both moms and dads over the family for a reason. Men bring strengths and talents to the family that wouldn't exist if they were absent.

Seek out your husband's strengths and encourage him to use them for the betterment of your children. This will not only improve your child's education, it will also help build stronger relationships between dads and their children.

Just Say No!

Criticism and Critique Wherever You Go

As a society, we put a lot of pressure on ourselves. No matter where we go, we seem to have someone giving us another task to do. At the dentist's office, we're told we need to floss. At the doctor's office, we're told me need to perform self-breast exams and have our yearly mammogram. At church, we're told we need to do family devotions, personal devotions, pray, tithe, and volunteer our time. We're asked to volunteer at cub scouts, coach our child's sports teams, attend board meetings, and sell various items to raise money.

We know we're supposed to eat supper as a family – and be sure that we prepare healthy, balanced meals that everyone will like. And food is obviously healthier if we make it all from scratch. We're supposed to exercise daily, plan date nights, keep the house clean, do laundry, and do the dishes. Oh, and don't forget spring cleaning the house. Does anyone else feel tired just reading this list?

As homeschool moms, we place even more pressure on ourselves. Not only are we responsible for all of the above activities; but, we are also in charge of creating fun, engaging lessons for each of our children, keeping up on our personal reading so that we are better able to teach, involving our kids in enough activities so that we won't be accused of having unsocialized children, reminding our kids to practice their instruments, helping them study for tests, and the list goes on and on.

There is no way we can do all of the tasks that are expected of us without going crazy. No one can live up to that kind of pressure! If you have chosen to homeschool, you are entering a season of life where you will need to learn to say "no" to some things without feeling guilty about it. With so many good opportunities out there, how do we know when to say "no?"

- **Is it a priority?** – Some things like exercise and eating healthy are important, whenever possible, in order to keep up your strength and to have the energy to carry on with life. Try to prioritize these items.

  Also, prioritizing your spiritual life is important – so finding time for prayer and devotions is also crucial. When you have young children, you may not be able to fit in family time, time with your children, and personal time. Do your best and God will be pleased with your efforts. You want to be sure to set as good of an example for your children as you can in this area.

- **Will your family be there anyway?** – If you are asked to volunteer as your child's coach and you would be attending their games anyway, then it's perfectly fine for you to accept. If you are asked to volunteer at church when the rest of your family will also be there, that's fine, too. Just be sure you aren't so busy volunteering that you never have any relaxation time for yourself. It's great to give back – but sometimes you are the one who needs to be fed.

If you can't answer "yes" to both of the above questions, then you may want to reconsider being involved in that activity at this time. This goes for dads as well as moms. The kids need you to be involved in their lives as well! Especially boys! Moms can raise boys but we can't teach them how to be men.

> *It's great to give back – but sometimes you are the one who needs to be fed.*

None of us enjoys the feeling that we are being criticized or critiqued. We all like to try to rise to the challenge when we are told about something else we "should" be doing.

Try not to take these words personally. People are trained to believe that their career is the most important in the whole world – and if you don't appear to agree with them, they will feel obligated to try to change your viewpoint.

If someone tells you how important it is for you to do "such and such", just say something non-committal like, "Oh, okay" or "Good to know." That type of answer is not argumentative and will allow you to continue on with your day without further lectures. Evaluate the advice later to determine whether it is something you want to add to your life or if it's something you can safely disregard… at least at this point in your life.

If you are talking with a friend or family member who is telling you about all of the wonderful things their child is doing and then appears to be critiquing your children, try be happy for them and let it go.

Don't accept the bait to compare your child to anyone else. Don't feel like you have to try to keep up with anyone else. Everyone's homeschool experience is unique and you are undoubtedly doing something else more effectively than is your friend.

We all have different strengths and weaknesses. When we compare ourselves to someone else, we are usually tempted to compare their strengths to our weaknesses. This is a great way to feel terrible about yourself or your family. Resist this temptation!

You need to put your family first during this busy time. Your children and your husband are your most important ministry. People who choose to homeschool their children are often used to being involved in many different activities. You aren't going to be able to be on every committee at church for awhile.

Once your children are grown, there will be plenty of time to jump in and get more involved. Relax and focus on your priorities. As long as we don't spread ourselves too thin, there really can be joy in the homeschool journey.

Stick With It

Our first year of having a son at the junior high level was an incredibly good year of homeschooling for us. Before the year began, I was extra nervous knowing that the intensity of his schooling was going to go up dramatically. I wasn't sure if he would rise to the challenge or if our lives would become mass chaos trying to juggle everything.

Even though the difficulty level definitely rose, my son did very well. This same son who used to struggle with writing anything down was suddenly writing papers which were several pages long. This son who would read for hours but struggled to spell even the easiest words was suddenly able to take his spelling tests with hardly any practice.

He began studying for and acing science tests that I would have had a hard time taking (even though we were studying the material together.) He would initiate deep conversations about logical fallacies. He enjoyed debating other people to defend his faith. He enjoyed filming movies and editing them on the computer. He even became proficient at giving speeches!

Not long ago, I was marveling with my husband at how much our son had matured, how enjoyable school had become, and how I was so glad we had stuck with homeschooling during the difficult years so that we could now enjoy the fruit of our labor.

Then it struck me that many people don't continue homeschooling past the elementary years. I personally know several homeschoolers who have put their kids into either a private or a public school for high school. In talking with people, they seem much more willing to accept that we will homeschool our children while they are young. A smaller percentage of people understand why we would continue homeschooling through the high school years. Why do they choose not to stick with it?

I think this is sad. I started homeschooling my boys when they were toddlers, just to be sure I could figure out what to do with them. I did tons of research and jumped in with both feet. I worked with my boys during the preschool years, teaching them how to count and how to read.

We transitioned to more book learning in the elementary grades and I saw them blossom. We had many frustrating days, yes, but we worked through the tough times and went on to see brighter stages of life. Once my boys were maturing and learning was coming easier for them, why would I want to enroll them in school and miss out on the best years of all?

Some parents don't feel capable of teaching their children high school level subjects. Let me reassure you that it is not up to you to be able to come up with the material on your own. Just like in younger grades, there is curriculum available for high school as well.

One change is that we may have been able to get away with not purchasing teacher's manuals, tests, or solution manuals when our children were younger. I would highly recommend we purchase these items as the subjects become more advanced. When my son took *Apologia General Science* [94]I would have been hard pressed to know whether or not some of his answers were correct without that solutions manual. With it, however, we did just fine.

> *Why would I want to enroll them in school and miss out on the best years of all?*

There are many other solutions available, as well, if you feel seriously intimidated by a subject. You may decide to hire a tutor, enroll your child in an online class, buy a computer class, buy teaching DVDs, or join a co-op.

Feel free to farm out a class if it is way above your comfort level. Don't feel that if one class is too much that you have to give up on homeschooling altogether. If you've been homeschooling your child all along, you should be able to help your child with the majority of their coursework.

One of the main goals of homeschooling is to teach children to be independent learners. As your child matures, you will want to do what you can to help guide your child into this type of learning. Help him to set his own schedules, let him read the

---

[94] Apologia General Science

materials and only help him as he has questions, let him help decide which courses he would like to take each year in order to reach his own goals, etc.

The more your child takes ownership of his learning, the better prepared he will be to do high school coursework – and college level classes as well, for that matter. If possible, you will want to try to read ahead in his books so that you can have intelligent conversations with him about what he is learning.

Another possibility is to team up with other homeschool families and have your children reading the same books and using the same coursework for a subject so that they can discuss what they're learning with each other. Book clubs are a great way for kids to learn the art of discussing serious subjects with their peers. There are great resources out there which contain questions you can ask them to facilitate their discussions. **Progeny Press Guides**[95] are a great way to help your children study a book in depth.

One of the most important goals of homeschooling isn't even related to their schoolwork. It is our desire to raise our children to have solid, moral character. It is much easier to influence our kids in this way if we are with them all day long.

When children attend school for the majority of their day, they are influenced more deeply by their peers than they are by their parents. This starts when they are quite young. Kindergarten and first grade students have a desire to fit in just as much as do older children. They begin to request designer clothing, to join in

---

[95] http://stores.progenypress.com/

mocking children who are being mocked by their friends, to value the things their teachers or their friends value over what their parents value, etc. Young children even begin to look for "boyfriend" and "girlfriend" relationships at way too young of an age.

By the time kids reach middle school and high school, they have been surrounded by peers long enough to have developed some extremely undesirable habits.

In my opinion, public high schools are entirely the wrong atmosphere in which to place our children. We've worked so hard to mould and shape our children when they are young. Why would we want to drop them into this type of hostile environment when we are mere yards away from the finish line?

Some who read this may be thinking that I plan to keep my children with me forever, protected in a sheltered cocoon so that they never have to experience life. That is certainly not the case. (See the chapter called "5 Vital Things You Can Do to "Harden Off" Your Son.") I am raising my sons to leave the nest, to be productive citizens, to be godly young men, to be faithful husbands and engaged fathers.

One day, they will be ready to enter the world and to fulfill their purpose in life. The world can be a cruel place – but I would contend that it is nowhere near as cruel as the artificially-created world that is a public school. If you are bullied in the workplace, you can quit your job. It's much harder to get away from bullying when you are in school. You can choose your work environment, at least to some degree. Kids don't have that luxury in school.

It is easier to avoid the pressures of sex, drugs, and alcohol at your job than it is at school. If we have done our jobs correctly, our children will stick out like a sore thumb at school. They should fit in much better in many work environments, as long as they make good career choices.

So, as you think ahead to the latter years of educating your children, please don't feel pressured to reinsert them into a traditional school. You can do it! You and your child can both rise to the occasion. And as you are able to experience your child maturing, learning, and growing, you will be blessed… if you just stick with it!

An Encouraging Word

Well, we've come to the end of this book. My hope is that reading these chapters has helped you to learn a little something about your son and how to best connect with and educate him. I pray that you come away from this experience with some fresh ideas and a renewed sense of hope.

Please don't think that you must do everything found within these chapters to be successful homeschooling your son. I'm not sure that's even possible. As Ecclesiastes 3:1 says, *"There is a time for everything, and a season for every activity under the heavens."*

Just as our sons go through various stages in life, we go through stages as well. There will be times when we are filled with energy and excitement and feel ready to take on the world. There will also be times when we feel beaten down and can barely put one foot in front of the other.

Our homeschool journeys will obviously reflect the way things are going in our lives… and that's alright.

Here is my advice to both make it through and enjoy your homeschool journey:
1. Ask God to guide you on your journey.
2. Don't beat yourself up.
3. Do your best and trust God for the rest.

You can do this, Homeschool Mom! Enjoy the journey!

Thank-you!

I wanted to personally thank you for purchasing **The Ultimate Guide to Homeschooling Boys**. I hope that reading this book has helped you to feel more confident and encouraged about homeschooling your son!

If you have a chance to leave a review on Amazon, I would really appreciate it. Your review could help other customers to also find and enjoy this product.

If you'd like to learn even more about homeschooling your son, I invite you to check out my blog: www.homeschool-your-boys.com. My desire is that my blog posts will encourage parents to better understand and connect with their sons. Boys can be loud and messy - but they are also a blessing! I also have a FREE weekly newsletter which contains all sorts of tips for teaching and enjoying your son. :)

If you ever have any problems or questions, feel free to email me at Michelle@homeschool-your-boys.com. You can also write to me if you'd like to share your victories!

Take care and I wish you and your child lots of fun and shared smiles as you continue to teach your child!

Michelle Caskey
www.homeschool-your-boys.com

Other Products by Michelle Caskey...

Learn and Grow: Hands-on Lessons for Active Preschoolers

Learn & Grow is packed with true hands-on learning for your preschooler, ages 2 – 4. The hands-on lessons are easy to follow, even for the non-experienced teacher.

Unique features:

- 130 daily lesson plans
- 26 weeks worth of lessons if done 5 days a week – 43 weeks worth if done 3 days a week – 65 weeks worth if done 2 days a week
- Over 700 individual, fully-planned activities
- Includes English, pre-math, history, science, geography, art, fine motor skills, gross motor skills, and literature
- Detailed lesson plans for each activity, including materials lists and step-by-step instructions for preparation as well as the steps necessary for teaching each lesson
- Most materials are easily found around the home or are simple to purchase – making teacher preparation quick and painless
- Lessons are great for boys AND girls!!!!!
- Can use concurrently with Teach Me About God: Hands-on Bible Lessons for Active Preschoolers

Learn more about Learn & Grow on my website:

www.homeschool-your-boys.com/learnandgrowpreschoolcurriculum.html

Teach Me About God: Hands-on Bible Lessons for Active Preschoolers

When first teaching your child about God, there are certain foundational concepts with which you should start such as "Who God is," "What God has done," "You can have a relationship with God," "You can be all God wants you to be," and "You can do all God wants you to do."

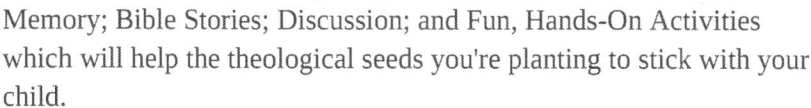

Our hands on preschool bible curriculum teaches these concepts using Scripture Memory; Bible Stories; Discussion; and Fun, Hands-On Activities which will help the theological seeds you're planting to stick with your child.

Unique features of Teach Me About God:

- 112 daily lesson plans
- Detailed lesson plans for each activity, including materials lists, step-by-step instructions for preparation, and the steps necessary for teaching each lesson
- Developed by a Sunday School and Awana preschool teacher with over 20 years of experience (that's ME)
- Most materials are easily found around the home or are simple to purchase – making teacher preparation quick and painless
- Includes an appendix with original illustrations
- Can use concurrently with our Learn and Grow: Hands-on Lessons for Active Preschoolers

Learn more about Teach Me About God on my website:

www.homeschool-your-boys.com/teachmeaboutgodbiblecurriculum.html

Time Capsule: Medieval England Unit Study

Time Capsule unit studies immerse your child in the daily life of whatever time period they are studying. They will get to wear the clothes, eat the food, perform the jobs, discover about the history, act in character, hear the music and the speech, learn about the geography, read about the people, and more. We try to do everything possible to make your child feel like they have been transported back to the Middle Ages without actually having a time machine!

The following subjects are covered in our Time Capsule: Medieval England Unit Study :

- Logic and Math
- History
- Reading and Literature
- Writing
- Photography
- Social Studies
- Drama
- Science
- Geography
- Arts and Crafts
- Learn to Draw
- Art Appreciation
- Music Appreciation and more

Learn More about Time Capsule: Medieval England on my website:

www.homeschool-your-boys.com/unitstudies.html

Dan and the Deer

Dan and the Deer is a Christian easy reader that you and your little ones will enjoy!

Dan loves apples! He's so excited when his parents help him buy and plant an apple tree in his own yard. Unfortunately, someone else also loves Dan's apple tree… and that someone is threatening to destroy it! What will Dan do? Will his tree survive?

Join Dan on this adventure. Will his tree survive? Will Dan learn how to rely on God when things aren't going as planned?

Dan and the Deer is an endearing children's picture book, written especially for you and your 0-7 year old children, with 22 colorful illustrations. The story is suitable as a read aloud book for preschoolers or a self-read book for beginning readers.

Learn More about Dan and the Deer on my website:

www.homeschool-your-boys.com/dan-and-the-deer-easy-reader.html

Lessons from the Garden: Why All the Weeds?

A Unique Retelling of Adam and Eve in the Garden of Eden that your Kids Will Love!

Dolly, a young dinosaur, loves to ask questions. No matter what she's doing, she is constantly asking questions. Whether she's helping her mom hang the laundry or eating dinner… Dolly has many questions running through her mind. One of the things she wonders about is why there are so many weeds in the garden. When she asks her grandpa this question, he takes her on a trip down memory lane to explain exactly why weeds came about.

Join Dolly on this adventure. What will happen after she discovers the origin of weeds? Will Dolly finally be satisfied with her grandpa's answer?

Lessons from the Garden: Why All the Weeds? is an endearing Easy Reader Christian Book, written especially for you and your 0-7 year old children, with 21 colorful illustrations. The story is suitable as a Read Aloud book for preschoolers or a self-read book for Beginning Readers.

Learn more about Why All the Weeds on my website:

www.homeschool-your-boys.com/easy-reader-christian-book.html

Made in the USA
San Bernardino, CA
05 October 2015